THE
LIFE & FAITH
FIELD GUIDE
FOR PARENTS

JOE CARTER

Property of
FAUQUIER COUNTY PUBLIC LIBRARY
11 Winchester Street
Warrenton, VA 20186

HARVEST HOUSE PUBLISHERS
EUGENE, OREGON

Unless otherwise indicated, all Scripture quotations are taken from the Holy Bible, New International Version®, NIV®. Copyright © 1973, 1978, 1984, 2011 by Biblica, Inc.® Used by permission. All rights reserved worldwide.

Scripture quotations marked CSB have been taken from the Christian Standard Bible®, Copyright 2017 by Holman Bible Publishers. Used by permission. Christian Standard Bible® and CSB® are federally registered trademarks of Holman Bible Publishers.

Verses marked NLT are taken from the Holy Bible, New Living Translation, copyright © 1996, 2004, 2015 by Tyndale House Foundation. Used by permission of Tyndale House Publishers, Inc., Carol Stream, Illinois 60188. All rights reserved.

Verses marked ESV are from The ESV® Bible (The Holy Bible, English Standard Version®), copyright © 2001 by Crossway, a publishing ministry of Good News Publishers. Used by permission. All rights reserved.

Verses marked KJV are taken from the King James Version of the Bible.

Verses marked NLV are taken from The New Life Version, © 1969 and 2003. Used by permission of Barbour Publishing, Inc., Uhrichsville, Ohio, 44683. All rights reserved.

Cover design by Bryce Williamson

Front cover photos © venimo, appleuzr, -VICTOR- / Getty

Back cover author photo by Teri Moy

Published in association with the literary agency of Wolgemuth & Associates. Inc.

The Life and Faith Field Guide for Parents
Copyright © 2019 Joe Carter
Published by Harvest House Publishers
Eugene, Oregon 97408
www.harvesthousepublishers.com

ISBN 978-0-7369-7448-6 (paperback)
ISBN 978-0-7369-7449-3 (eBook)

Library of Congress Cataloging-in-Publication Data

Names: Carter, Joe, author.
Title: The life and faith field guide for parents / Joe Carter.
Description: Eugene, Oregon : Harvest House Publishers, [2019] | Includes
   bibliographical references.
Identifiers: LCCN 2018013037 (print) | LCCN 2018036355 (ebook) | ISBN
   9780736974493 (ebook) | 9780736974486¬(paperback)
Subjects: LCSH: Parenting—Religious aspects—Christianity—Study and
   teaching. | Parenting—Religious aspects—Christianity. | Child
   rearing—Religious aspects—Christianity—Study and teaching. | Child
   rearing—Religious aspects. | Christian education of children.
Classification: LCC BV4529 (ebook) | LCC BV4529 .C4268 2019 (print) | DDC
   248.8/45—dc23
LC record available at https://lccn.loc.gov/2018013037

All rights reserved. No part of this publication may be reproduced, stored in a retrieval system, or transmitted in any form or by any means—electronic, mechanical, digital, photocopy, recording, or any other—except for brief quotations in printed reviews, without the prior permission of the publisher.

Printed in the United States of America

18 19 20 21 22 23 24 25 26 / BP-RD / 10 9 8 7 6 5 4 3 2 1

To
The Boy Scout Handbook

CONTENTS

Why This Book Is Dedicated to *The Boy Scout Handbook* . .   9

1. How to Learn So You Can Teach   15

Part 1: Skills and Habits for Bible Engagement

2. How to Prepare Your Child to Read the Bible   25

3. How to Read the Bible (Elementary)   27

4. How to Read the Bible (Advanced)   35

5. How to See Jesus in the Old Testament   43

6. How to Study the Bible   47

7. How to Interpret the Bible   53

8. How to Apply Scripture to Your Life   57

9. How to Meditate on God's Word   63

10. How to Memorize Bible Verses   67

11. How to Memorize Entire Books of the Bible   69

12. How to Read the Entire Bible   73

13. How to Memorize the Biblical Narrative   79

Part 2: Skills and Habits for Interacting with God

14. How to Pray   89

15. How to Be Obedient to God   93

16. How to Overcome Sin   97

17. How to Develop Trust in God   103

Part 3: Skills and Habits for Interacting with Other People

18. How to Handle Criticism   111

19. How to Stand Up for Yourself   115

20. How to Say You're Sorry   119

21. How to Forgive   123

Part 4: Skills and Habits for Discernment and Decision-Making

22. How to Develop Your Conscience 129
23. How to Know God's Will for Your Life 133
24. How to Make Better Decisions 137
25. How to Develop Biblical Discernment 141

Part 5: Skills and Habits for Mental and Physical Health

26. How to Sleep 147
27. How to Manage Stress 151
28. How to Handle Loss and Grief 157
29. How to Deal with Fear and Anxiety 161
30. How to Develop a Healthy Body Image 167

Part 6: Skills and Habits for Character Development

31. How to Develop Godly Grit 173
32. How to Tame Your Tongue 177
33. How to Develop Virtuous Habits 183
34. How to Change Negative Habits 187

Part 7: Skills and Habits for Engaging Culture

35. How to Look at Art 193
36. How to Listen to Music 199
37. How to Watch a Movie 203
38. How to Consume the News 209

Part 8: Skills and Habits for Learning

39. How to Study. 217
40. How to Become a Better Learner 223
41. How to Memorize Almost Anything 227
42. How to Focus. 237

Part 9: Skills and Habits for Managing Conflict

43. How to Handle Conflict 243
44. How to Deal with Bullying and Harassment 247
45. How to Handle Family Conflict. 253
46. How to Handle Peer Pressure 261

Part 10: Skills and Habits for Evangelism

47. How to Start a Conversation About the Gospel 269
48. How to Defend the Faith 273
49. How to Tell a Bible Story 277
50. How to Share the Gospel 281

Recommended Resources 285
Notes 287

Why This Book Is Dedicated to
The Boy Scout Handbook

In the medieval era, books were often dedicated to a king or queen. Today, most books are dedicated to the author's spouse, children, or colleagues. This book, however, is different. It's dedicated not to a notable individual but to another book—*The Boy Scout Handbook*.

In 1970, on my tenth birthday, my grandmother gave me a copy of the newly released ninth edition of *The Boy Scout Handbook*. I was in fifth grade and not yet old enough to join the local Boy Scout troop. Nonetheless, I read the *Handbook* cover to cover and attempted to apply every page to my life. The *Handbook* became not only a guide to living in my rural Texas surroundings but also a map showing me how to become the person I wanted to be.

I believed that something about being a Boy Scout would make me a better Christian. I wanted to embody the 12 points of the Scout Law because I sensed their connection with what I was learning in Sunday school. I wanted to be trustworthy (Psalm 101:7), loyal (Ruth 1:16), helpful (Leviticus 19:18), brave (1 Chronicles 28:20), and so on.

I didn't quite understand how learning to tie knots and build campfires would make me a better person, much less a better Christian, but I did see some connection in the lives of the young Eagle Scouts in my hometown. I took 20 more years to recognize *The Boy Scout Handbook* was effective because it was a manual for building a moral worldview.

When the ninth edition was released in 1970, cultural critic Paul Fussell called it a "compendia of good sense":

The good sense is psychological and ethical as well. Indeed, this hand-book is among the very few remaining popular repositories of something like classical ethics, deriving from Aristotle and Cicero...The constant moral theme is the inestimable benefits of looking objectively outward and losing consciousness of self in the work to be done.[1]

Much of the success of Scouting is due to the ethical worldview it presents, a worldview that is admittedly secular but nevertheless (mostly) compatible with Christianity. Because it is not founded on biblical principles, though, the worldview of Scouting is ultimately lacking as a guide to life. Still, when I searched for alternatives, I discovered that many books founded on biblical principles presented a less effective guide to life than Scouting. What were those books missing?

Scouting emphasizes two important truths we can borrow: (1) To build a strong character, we need not only to acquire ethical knowledge but also to develop practical skills and virtuous habits, and (2) to learn a skill or habit, we need to be taught by someone who understands the concept and knows how to teach it.

The purpose of this book is to help you learn and develop these elements so you can empower your children to form a godly character and a Christian worldview.

To help you achieve this goal, this book will show you how to solve what I call the "fifth-grade math problem" and the "100-book / 1,000-hour problem."

Character Education and the Fifth-Grade Math Problem

Several years ago, the Fox network aired a quiz show called *Are You Smarter Than a 5th Grader?* On the show, an adult contestant attempted to answer ten questions (plus a final bonus question) based on content from elementary school textbooks. The first two questions were based on first-grade level, the second two on second-grade, and so on until the final two were on the fifth-grade level. The prize for answering the first question correctly was $1,000, and those who answered all ten plus the bonus question walked away with $1,000,000.

Almost every adult you know completed the fifth grade, so you might expect dozens of people to win a million dollars. But in fact, only two contestants did:

a Nobel Prize–winning physicist and the superintendent of public schools for the state of Georgia.

Why was the challenge difficult for adults who had learned the content when they were children? That's a question parents ask themselves when trying to teach their own children fifth-grade math. You may have learned elementary math well enough to function as an adult (what I call "learning to apply"), but knowing it well enough to *teach* it to a child (what I refer to as "learning to teach") is surprisingly challenging.

When you approach topics in a learn-to-apply manner (especially topics that don't interest you), you typically learn them only superficially. You learn the topic *just enough* to apply it the way you will probably need to (which may be nothing more than regurgitating it for a school exam). But when you approach a topic in a learn-to-teach manner, you recognize the need to understand the concepts well enough to adequately explain them to others.

Most of us never approached fifth-grade math in a learn-to-teach manner, so we now struggle to pass on to our children what little knowledge we retained about multiplying and dividing fractions. Unfortunately, what is true for elementary math is also true for topics associated with Christian character and worldview formation. Even parents with a doctorate in Christian ethics may not know how to teach those topics to their own children.

But knowing how to teach the topic is only the first problem we face. The second is a matter of time.

Busy Parents and the 100-Book / 1,000-Hour Problem

Thirteen years and six months after my grandmother gave me a copy of *The Boy Scout Handbook*, I became a father. Like most first-time fathers, I was scared to death I didn't know enough to keep my daughter alive, much less to help her grow into a fully functioning, mature Christian adult.

But I thought I knew where to find the answer to my deficiencies—I'd find it in books.

I've always been the "bookish" type, and I particularly enjoy books on advice and self-help. I figured anything I needed to know about being a parent could be found in a book. All I needed was to discover which books held the secret knowledge of parenthood, and I'd be halfway to becoming Father of the Year.

I quickly realized I was partially right. A wealth of useful, practical advice for parents is available from wise and mature Christians who have written books revealing many of the secrets of parenting. The problem is, most of those books contain only one to three "secrets." For example, I might find a superb book explaining how to watch and evaluate movies from a Christian perspective. But I often needed to read the entire book to gain those one or two important insights.

And evaluating movies was merely one of hundreds of skills I needed to know as a parent! At ten hours a book, I would spend about a thousand hours just to learn the material needed to teach my child 50 life skills. What busy parent has time for that?

That is exactly why I've written this book—to save you time.

And What Makes Me an Expert?

I'm not an expert.

I'm not an educator. I'm an elder at my church and have taught in our children's ministry, but I've never been a youth pastor. I have an MBA, but not an MDiv. I have a daughter but no special expertise on children. What then qualifies me to write a book that teaches *you* how to teach *your* kids?

The surprising (and hopefully compelling) answer is that I'm a Christian journalist.

Andy Crouch, a former executive editor at *Christianity Today*, provides a helpful explanation of the calling of the Christian journalist. Crouch says the role of the journalist is to "make complicated things clear, quickly, for people who could be doing something else, in the service of truth."

Crouch notes the vocational calling of journalists differs from the roles of both scholars and teachers. Scholars make clear things complicated by uncovering the complexity at the heart of physical and social reality. Teachers make complicated issues clear but often have more time and space to do so. The journalist, in contrast, attempts to communicate complicated issues clearly and quickly using relatively few words.

That is why a journalist is the right person to write this book. We journalists perform our tasks for people—in this case, parents—who are busy doing other important things. My role is like that of a short-order cook at a diner. You could make a chicken fried steak dinner yourself—planning the menu, assembling the ingredients, and cooking the food—but sometimes having someone do it for you makes sense.

In writing this book, I've read a couple hundred relevant articles and books, spent hundreds of hours searching for the information you need, distilled it down to its essential points, and attempted to explain it as simply as possible. I want not only to save you time but also show you how you can rapidly learn this content—and learn it in a way you can not only understand but also teach to children.

How This Book Works

This book contains 50 skills and habits grouped into several broad categories. Almost all these skills and habits are interconnected, and many build the foundation for other skills and habits.

For example, learning how to focus or how to study may not seem directly relevant to character formation. But those skills have the same function as tying knots and building fires have for the Boy Scouts—they are essential for other skills we need to acquire, such as learning how to study Scripture or defend our beliefs. Too often, we struggle to develop and apply core skills and habits because we lack these indirectly related metaskills.

These 50 skills and habits are not the only ones your child will need to develop in life, but each has been chosen because it is either a core skill or a key metaskill necessary for developing a Christian character and worldview. Each chapter includes a brief explanation of a concept as well as tips and techniques for learning or teaching it quickly.

Whom This Book Is For

Because this book takes a "train the trainer" approach, it is primarily for Christian adults who want to shape the character and worldview of a child or teenager. In this way it is less like *The Boy Scout Handbook* and more like *The Scoutmaster Handbook*. It is a guide for adults who guide children.

Older teens and college students may also gain from reading this book, as would adults who feel they need remedial instruction in character formation. (That's nothing to be ashamed of; many of us never learned these skills and habits when we were children.)

Although most references in this book are to parents, many of the habits can be taught by anyone who has an influential role in a child's life, such as an older sibling, aunt or uncle, pastor, or teacher. If God has put you in a child's life to influence their worldview, this book is for you.

The 20 to 80 Percent Objective

Many books overpromise and underdeliver, so I want to be straightforward with you about what you should expect to gain from reading this guide.

My assumption is you won't find every part of this book useful. Some features you'll already know, some you won't care about, and some you'll think I do an inadequate job of explaining. Based on this, my objective is to achieve a success rate of between 20 and 80 percent. I truly believe readers who find 80 percent of this content to be useful and take the time to apply it can transform a child's life. That's more than any author can ask for. But even if you only find 20 percent of the material applicable, I think the results will be worth the time and effort you spent reading this book. And that's about the least any reader can ask for.

If that's enough for you, turn the page, and let's get started.

1

How to Learn So You Can Teach

This book came about because of the word "whimsical." And "facetious." And "déjà vu." And a hundred other terms my daughter had once asked me, "Dad, what does this word mean?"

I knew what the words meant—or I thought I did. I could understand them when I saw them in a book. I could use them in a sentence. I could even spell them (most of them, anyway). But when my own child asked me what those words meant, I couldn't explain them in a way she could understand. I knew the words in a way that allowed me to function, and yet I couldn't pass on the knowledge I had acquired over a lifetime of reading and talking.

In other words, I didn't truly know those words. As the famous educator Mortimer Adler said, "The person who says he knows what he thinks but cannot express it usually does not know what he thinks."[1]

I soon realized this problem wasn't limited to vocabulary words. I also couldn't explain how to study the Bible or deal with peer pressure. I couldn't explain how to share the gospel, manage stress, or deal with bullies. I had acquired hundreds of life skills that I couldn't explain and pass along to my daughter.

No one had told me when I became a parent this would be a problem.

Maybe it's not a problem for all parents. Maybe many moms and dads intuitively understand how to pass along such knowledge to their progeny. Even so, I suspect there are also a lot like me who, even if they had learned the information for themselves (which isn't a certainty), don't have the first clue about how to teach it to their own children.

By the time I figured out how to solve this problem, my daughter was already an adult. (Now I have to wait till I have grandchildren to share what I know.) Hopefully, you still have time to learn the simple process of how to learn. Once you master this technique, you'll be able to teach almost any concept to your children.

Learn to Teach with the Feynman Technique

Science educator David Goodman once asked the brilliant Nobel Prize–winning physicist Richard Feynman to explain a certain puzzling phenomenon. Feynman said, "I'll prepare a freshman lecture on it." But a few days later, said Goodman, Feynman came back and said, "You know, I couldn't do it. I couldn't reduce it to the freshman level. That means we really don't understand it."[2]

Notice Feynman claimed not only that *he* didn't genuinely understand the concept but also that the *entire scientific community* didn't understand the concept. He had a firm belief that once we truly understand an idea we should be able to explain it in simple terms to non-experts.

Feynman became known as the Great Explainer because he intentionally learned a subject in a way that allowed him to teach it to those who didn't share his expertise. His method is now known as the Feynman Technique and can be used to learn the key concepts behind the habits and skills in this book. This method helps you learn these concepts, retain the knowledge indefinitely, and pass on the information to your children in a way they can understand.

Here are the five steps of the Feynman Technique.

1. *Pick a concept you want to understand and start studying it.* First write down the concept you want to learn in a notebook. Next, do the minimal amount of reading and research necessary for you to understand what the concept is about, and then write what you think you should know about the topic in the notebook. At this stage, you don't need to waste a lot of time trying to learn everything about the topic. You only need to know the core components necessary to understand and explain the concept.

Regarding the habits and skills listed in this book, I've already compiled all this information. Each entry provides a brief overview of what you need to know about the concepts involved to learn the habit or skill. This will often be enough for the purposes of learning to teach your child, but additional resources may also be needed if you are completely unfamiliar with the subject.

2. *Prepare to teach your topic to a child.* Using these key elements, write an explanation of the concept in your own words using simple language. You can make your explanation as detailed as you think is necessary, but generally the shorter and simpler you can make it, the easier it will be for you to understand and teach the material. Check it against your notes or other resources to see if any essential elements are missing from your explanation.

You can also do this step by making a voice recording (for example, using your smartphone) and having it transcribed electronically. Regardless of the method you choose, do not skip this step—it's essential for learning to teach the material.

Seriously. Do not skip this step.

Because this step takes additional work, you may be tempted to assume it's not necessary. It's easy to tell yourself that since you understand the material you'll be able to explain it to your child when the time comes. This assumption is often why we fail to learn in a way that allows us to teach. As Feynman once said, "The first principle is that you must not fool yourself—and you are the easiest person to fool."

Once you've put the concept in your own words and checked it against your notes, try to explain it to another adult. Ask them to think about the explanation from the point of view of an elementary school student. Have them provide critical feedback and pay attention to the areas where they believe you've used words that are overly complicated.

3. *Locate your knowledge gap.* Identify the parts of your explanation that are complex, incomplete, or otherwise unclear. These are likely to be the areas where you don't truly understand the concept. Review your notes and the source material once again and, if necessary, do some additional reading on the topic. Rewrite your explanation to fill in these knowledge gaps.

4. *Use analogies.* Look over your explanation and search for complex terms and concepts you can simplify by using analogies. God commonly uses analogies—metaphors and similes—to explain complex ideas to us in Scripture. We are designed to learn by connecting new concepts to knowledge we already have, so using analogies is one of the most effective ways to teach new ideas to children.

5. *Explain the concept to your child.* This is the definitive test of whether you've learned the information well enough to teach it. If your child is confused, you may need to do more reading or refine your analogies. Always begin

with the assumption the problem is with *your own understanding or preparation* and not with the child's ability to comprehend the concept. However, if you've effectively taught the material to other children, a genuine communication gap may be hindering your ability to teach this child this concept. Don't worry. This is not only normal, it is nearly inevitable on occasion when teaching these skills and habits.

Sometimes we simply can't transmit what we know to our own children. Don't be discouraged! Just seek out someone else to teach that subject. Sometimes something just "clicks" with a child when they hear the same explanation from another parent or even another adult. You'll have plenty of opportunities to teach your child other areas or skill clusters, so don't get frustrated when you don't fully connect.

If It's Easy, Why Can't You Do It for Me?

The Feynman Technique is a powerful and effective way to easily learn and teach concepts. You might wonder why this book doesn't provide a detailed list of simple, analogy-filled explanations and ready-made scripts parents could read to their own children to teach these concepts, habits, and skills. That's a reasonable question. But that approach would make the process less effective for three reasons.

First, you need to know this material to be an effective model. If you want your child to develop a robust biblical worldview, you need to be a living example of how to display that worldview in day-to-day life. This means you must first develop the worldview you want to pass along to your children.

For example, what's the best way to help children develop a love for church? Some parents who don't attend church themselves believe they can drop off their kids at Sunday school or vacation Bible school, and the children will learn enough to follow Jesus. But these children receive the message that church isn't a priority for Mom and Dad so it must not be important for their lives either. Similarly, if your children get the impression they are expected to develop a worldview but it's not an important part of your life, they won't take it seriously regardless of how hard you try to teach them.

Second, you need to know this material because you'll need to teach it repeatedly. Remember when you were potty training your child, and all you had to do was show them how to use the toilet one time and they caught on immediately? Of course you don't—potty training is *never* that easy.

The same is true for the skills and habits needed for worldview formation. On a few rare occasions, you will teach a child a concept in this book, and they learn it immediately and completely and apply it consistently for the rest of their lives. But more often you'll have to repeat the lessons over and over and over...until you feel like your brain will turn to mush if you have to explain it *one more time*. (Fortunately, in the history of parenting, no brains have actually turned to mush because of repetition.)

Also, teachable moments often occur when you don't have access to learning materials, like this book. If the material is in your head, though, you will have it ready whenever and wherever it is needed (although you may not always have the patience you'll need to teach a concept for the umpteenth time).

The third reason standardized scripts don't work is that every child is unique. You've spent more time with your child than most other people and probably know them better than anyone else does. You've likely also learned through a frustratingly long process of trial and error how your child learns and the best way for them to retain new knowledge and acquire new skills. That's why the "Tips for Training Children" in most of the entries includes broad-based, adaptable suggestions rather than narrow, detailed activities.

God has given you the authority to teach your child as well as—if you are willing to make the effort—the ability to teach them these habits so they'll become more adept at living like a follower of Jesus. If you will take the time to learn to teach your own children, they will be much more likely to develop these abilities than if you used a generic, scripted approach.

Making the Process Easier

Are you feeling a bit overwhelmed, thinking this will require more time and energy than you can possibly muster? Fear not. Here are a few ways to make the process easier—and even enjoyable!

Share the workload. Ideally, the character and worldview of every Christian child would be shaped by two parents who had fully developed a gospel-centered worldview, and by four grandparents who shared that perspective, and by a church with dozens of people willing to help. Unfortunately, we don't live in such a world.

Because of death or divorce, you may not have a spouse to carry some of the load. Or the child's other parent may be unable or unwilling to help. Your extended family may not live close enough to influence your children. You might even be a teacher who is filling a parental role the child is lacking. Whatever the case may be, you may begin to feel you are being expected to bear this burden alone.

But you are not alone. Not only is Jesus there for you (Matthew 11:28), your brothers and sisters in Christ are also called to help you carry this burden (Galatians 6:2). Ask for the help you need.

Although you will want and need to learn these skills and habits for yourself, you can enlist others in developing additional resources and materials you need to learn and teach. Explain this process to your family, friends, and fellow church members. Ask them if they would be willing to provide their own notes on how to use these concepts to teach your child.

You can also divide the workload among numerous families. The other parents you know from church, your neighborhood school, social media, or a homeschooling co-op likely share your general perspective. Because the explanations they prepare for their own children will likely resonate with yours, you can often save time by sharing notes, tips, techniques, and explanations.

But even if you have no one else to help you learn this material, don't get discouraged. The first few times you try to put concepts into your own words, you'll find the process challenging. Stick with it. After working through the process half a dozen times, you'll find it becomes quicker and easier. You'll even begin to look for analogies and ways of simplifying terminology for concepts you haven't yet started working on.

You'll likely also find this process is helpful for preparing to explain ideas not covered in this book, such as when children ask why a relative died or where babies come from. Once you get in the habit of simplifying concepts, it becomes almost second nature.

How to Supercharge Your Learning

The Feynman Technique is a powerful tool, but two additional steps make it exponentially more effective.

The first is to pray before every step in the learning process. Ask God specifically to give you the wisdom and understanding you need to learn the concepts behind the skills and habits we'll use to develop a biblical worldview. As the apostle James wrote, "If any of you lacks wisdom, let him ask God, who gives generously to all without reproach, and it will be given him" (James 1:5 ESV).

The second additional step is to commit to a specific plan for applying this technique on a regular basis—and sticking to it for at least a year. At a minimum, make a commitment to work on this project for 15 minutes every day, 6 days a week. No matter how busy our lives may become, we can find a quarter of an hour out of the 24 we are given daily to make time to learn.

But what can be accomplished in that amount of time? More than you might expect. Let's calculate how much you could accomplish with this minimal effort.

The average adult reads prose text at 250 to 300 words per minute. In 15 minutes, you could read 3,750 to 4,500 words. In less than 6 months (156 days), you would spend 2,340 minutes reading. Multiply that times 250 words per minute, and you get 585,000 words. The average nonfiction book contains 35,000 to 80,000 words (this book is rather long at 70,000 words), so in 156 days you could read the equivalent of 7 to 16 books.

Now imagine you spend the other 6 months of the year learning specific concepts and writing out explanations. (Of course, you would do this as you went along, but for this example we'll assume the reading and writing process are separated.) Let's say you take about 30 minutes to write about a concept since you've already read about it extensively. Over the next 156 days, you'd be able to create explanations for 78 concepts.

Now consider how much you could learn by applying this technique for only 15 minutes a day over several years. In 5 years you'd have read the equivalent of about 75 books and produced 390 concepts. In 10 years you'd have read the equivalent of 150 books and produced 780 concepts. And in 15 years you could finish the equivalent of 225 books and learn 1,170 concepts. All with only 15 minutes of effort a day.

That's the power of consistently applying small incremental steps, even for brief amounts of time. The amount of learning and growth you can achieve even in a year is astounding. And you can pass on that learning to your kids.

If you need even more motivation, just ask yourself one question: "Aren't my children worth the effort?"

PART 1

SKILLS AND HABITS FOR BIBLE ENGAGEMENT

How to Prepare Your Child to Read the Bible

Why do we teach our children to read?

You've probably never given the question much thought. After all, no one has ever asked you, "Do you want your child to learn to read, or do you think it's unnecessary?" (If your child's teacher asked that question, you'd likely be looking for a new school.)

We consider literacy to be so obviously beneficial to our lives, we'd never consider *not* teaching our kids how to read. But we don't give much thought to *why* we teach them to read. If you're a Christian parent, the answer to this question should be obvious: so they can read the Bible.

The Bible is the most important text produced in the history of the world. It's the most important text your child will ever read. "Since Moses descended from the mountain with two loose-leaf stones under his arms, all literature can be divided into two genres," says Tony Reinke. "Genre A: The Bible…Genre B: All other books."[1]

The fact that learning to read the Bible will also help your children read traffic signs, text messages, and *War and Peace* is certainly beneficial. But every other type of reading is of secondary importance to reading the Bible.

Some missionaries spend years or even decades learning how to teach literacy to unreached people. Why do they do that? Primarily, to give those people the tools they need to read the Word of God for themselves.

As Christian parents—missionaries to our own children—we want our kids to know how to read so they too can one day read the Bible for themselves. This mindset about teaching can lead to long-lasting benefits for your children. Instead of viewing the literacy process as the means to reach the goal of reading, think of it instead as the means by which your child reaches the goal of *reading the Bible*.

This may appear to be a trivial distinction. After all, children who learn to read will likely be able to read the Bible. While that is true, a profound shift occurs when we teach reading for the *primary* goal of reading Scripture.

Whatever stage your child is at in their literacy education—whether they're an infant learning words for the first time or a high school student learning vocabulary terms for the SAT—consider this to be your objective: to shape their reading so they can better read the literature that falls into "Genre A."

When the goal of reading is to read the Bible, you will think differently about a child's education in literacy. You'll begin to recognize small ways you can shift the focus, especially their early reading efforts, in a way that prepares them to become better readers of God's Word. (They'll also gain the additional benefit of being better readers of all types of text.)

In 1940, the American philosopher and educator Mortimer J. Adler wrote *How to Read a Book*.[2] Adler said his book was for readers whose "main purpose in reading books is to gain increased understanding." Because this is an explicitly biblical purpose for reading (Proverbs 4:7) and because Adler's guidelines apply to reading the Great Books of the Western World (a course Adler helped develop), his method can help us prepare our children to read the Greatest Book. In the next two entries—"How to Read the Bible (Elementary)" and "How to Read the Bible (Advanced)"—we'll apply some of Adler's insights to learning to read Scripture.

3

How to Read the Bible (Elementary)

The first phase of reading is elementary reading. Adler notes that the four stages of this level roughly align with the early years of the school curriculum:

- Stage 1: Reading readiness—the ability to follow directions, a capacity for sustained attention, and so on.
- Stage 2: Word mastery—the ability to recognize and read basic words, the ability to use context clues to discern meaning of words, and more.
- Stage 3: Functional literacy—rapid progress in vocabulary building, greater ability to use context clues for finding meaning, and the like.
- Stage 4: Advanced literacy—refinement and enhancement of previously acquired skills.

Stage 1: Reading Readiness

The goal of this first stage is to develop Bible-reading readiness by creating in the child a desire to learn to read so they can read the Bible for themselves. Even before the child learns the alphabet, you can prepare their heart and mind to hear God's Word by (1) encouraging them to imitate your reading habits and (2) exposing them to the stories and imagery of the Bible.

A primary way children "learn to desire" is through imitation. They are constantly observing adults to discover what behavior they want to imitate. A child asks for a sip of your coffee not only because they are curious about how it tastes but also because they associate coffee drinking with maturity, with being an adult. They observe Mom and Dad doing something children don't do, and they assume it must therefore be desirable. Because of this urge to imitate, it is imperative your child frequently observes you reading the Bible. You want your child to associate Bible reading with maturity, specifically a habit of mature Christians.

You're probably thinking, especially if you have a toddler, you can't get much productive Bible reading done if your children are around. This is most certainly true. It's difficult to accomplish almost any productive tasks around infants, much less a task that requires as much sustained attention as Bible reading. So you'll need to sacrifice some of your time. You'll need to find quiet time where you can be alone with the Lord to read his Word *and* find time when your child can see you reading Scripture. The latter times are as much for your child's edification as for your own.

Another way to increase your child's desire for the Bible is to expose them to its stories and imagery. In previous generations this meant reading the adults' Bible translation out loud to children. Unfortunately, this often had the opposite effect of what was intended. When children hear language they don't understand, they can grow bored and develop negative associations that cause them to want to avoid such material in the future.

One solution is to use a paraphrase—a Bible version that preserves the meaning, if not the text, in language that is more easily understandable. Today we have a broad range of complete Bible paraphrases for children, including the International Children's Bible and the Easy-to-Read Version.

Another option, particularly suited for preschool children, is to read from collections of selected Bible stories, such as *The Complete Illustrated Children's Bible*. Because these books are anthologies, they can't provide the same scope and grandeur as a paraphrase or translation that contains all God's Word. Still, such books do provide the essential benefit of getting younger children excited about engaging with Scripture. At this phase of development, that is one of the most important long-term goals we hope to achieve.

Stage 2: Word Mastery

At this stage children are broadening their vocabulary by learning the meaning of new words. For most types of reading, this process comes from being told the meaning or discovering it from the context of the story. For Bible reading, though, there is a way to develop word mastery that can be enjoyable for both you and your child: Take them outdoors.

Psalms 19 states, "The heavens declare the glory of God; the skies proclaim the work of his hands. Day after day they pour forth speech; night after night they reveal knowledge" (verses 1-2). God speaks to us through this "general revelation" as well as through the "special revelation" of the Bible. Because they are both forms of God's truth, we should be attuned to both types of revelation. Paying close attention to general revelation can enrich our reading of Scripture. Scott Steltzer explains:

> A heart attuned to creation's song is better positioned to comprehend and cherish the truths of Scripture. This is true even with the simplest of terms. Humor me for a moment and read this list aloud to yourself. Shut your eyes after each word and let your mind make the biblical connections:
>
> Sheep. Green grass. Stars. Sun. Tree. Branch. Seed. Root. Light. Sky. Rock. Stream. Sand. Wave. Storm. Cloud. Lightning. Thunder. Mountain. Field. Cliff. Dust. Stone. Locust. Flower. Sparrow. Desert. Sea. Fire. Water.
>
> Since we understand God more deeply through both his Word and his world, withdrawing from creation hampers our understanding of God.[1]

Of course, a child can learn what sheep, locust, or mustard seeds are simply by reading about them. But they will develop a deeper appreciation when they experience nature firsthand—running their fingers through the wool of a lamb, hearing the sound of locusts in the fields, or feeling the smallness of a mustard seed on their tongue.

Going on a nature walk or to a petting zoo is not merely an entertaining diversion. These activities are means of experiencing the general revelation of nature that can have a lifelong influence on how your son or daughter reads the Bible.

Stage 3: Functional Literacy

At this stage the child begins shifting from a children's Bible to an adult translation and becomes capable of understanding the larger moral and theological themes of the text. While we should encourage them to dig into the meaning of Scripture, we shouldn't forget they are still developing their literacy skills. In a rush to help them develop an adult understanding of God's Word, we may miss out on an opportunity to provide them with a knowledge base that can improve their Bible reading for decades to come.

This stage is an ideal time to expand their basic knowledge of Bible facts, information necessary for developing a nuanced understanding of the context and message of Scripture. Yet too often we overlook teaching these facts because we don't know them ourselves. We are likely to have been taught the same process of "read first, seek understanding later." But by teaching kids basic Bible facts at the elementary reading phase—a time when they are eager to acquire such knowledge—we provide them with a firm foundation of contextual knowledge. Since we want them to read the Bible for the rest of their lives, having this understanding of facts from an early age can enrich their later readings.

Tips for Training Children

Because you'll be teaching this material, you may need a refresher about such Bible facts yourself. Start by using a Bible handbook (see the recommended resources section) to develop a basic familiarity with biblical information.

Birds, Beasts, and Plants

From birds to dogs (Genesis 1:20; Revelation 22:15) and from seed-bearing plants to the tree of life (Genesis 1:11; Revelation 22:19), the Bible is filled with references to flora and fauna. Now that children can identify various plants and animals mentioned in the Bible, skills they gained in the reading readiness stage, they are ready to learn more about important ways plants and animals fit into the biblical story.

Some passages of the Bible, such as the story of Noah, make more sense when you become familiar with the significance of plants and animals. For instance, sailors the world over used doves, ravens, and other birds to help them find and navigate toward land. A raven will fly directly toward land, so its line of flight can be used as a guide. Doves have a limited ability for sustained flight, so they can be used to determine the location of a landing site. If the dove returns, no landing site is in close range (see Genesis 8:6-12).

The Calendar of Ancient Israel

In the Old Testament, people kept time by the cycles of the moon rather than a solar calendar like we use today. Kids don't necessarily need to know the names of the months in this system, but by learning about the lunar calendar, they will discover that the farm season and festivals (both of which play a significant role in the story of the Israelites) don't necessarily fall on the same days every year as they would in our calendar system.

Parallel Civilizations

Some of the most powerful civilizations in history (including the Assyrian, Babylonian, and Roman) play important roles in the story and timeline of the Bible. Older children should have at least a rudimentary knowledge about each of these civilizations and be able to explain how they overlap with the Bible story. Their understanding doesn't need to be complex or in-depth. For example, simply knowing the Romans controlled the biblical lands during the time of Jesus and the apostles can help kids later when they learn about the Roman Empire.

Measures

Like the American system of measuring by inches and feet, the Bible uses human-based measurements. Here are some helpful approximate measurements to know.

- Finger—the width of the average man's finger, or 3/4 inch (Jeremiah 52:21)
- Handbreadth—4 fingers, or 3 inches (Exodus 25:25)
- Span—3 handbreadths, or 9 inches (Exodus 28:16)
- Cubit—2 spans, or 18 inches (Matthew 6:27 KJV)
- Fathom—4 cubits, or 6 feet (Acts 27:28 ESV)
- Reed—6 cubits, or 9 feet (Ezekiel 40:5 ESV)
- Furlong—1/8 mile, or 660 feet (Revelation 14:20 KJV)

- Sabbath day's journey—3/5 mile (Acts 1:12)
- Day's journey—20 miles (1 Kings 19:4)[2]

Weights

Unfortunately, biblical weights aren't as intuitive as measurements. But for most purposes it's enough to know these comparisons.

- Gerah—roughly half a teaspoon, or 1/50 ounce (Ezekiel 45:12)
- Bekah—10 gerahs, or 1/5 ounce (about the weight of a US quarter) (Genesis 24:22)
- Shekel—2 bekahs, or 2/5 ounces (Exodus 30:23)
- Mina—50 shekels, or 1.25 pounds (about the weight of a soccer ball) (Ezra 2:69)
- Talent—60 minas, or 75 pounds (about the average weight of an 11-year-old boy) (Ezra 8:26)[3]

Currency

Most of the currencies in the Bible are based on the weight of silver or gold. Kids don't necessarily need to know the exact values, but it's useful to know the relations between units (for example, 50 shekels equal 1 mina, and 60 minas equal 1 talent). They should also know a denarius was equal to a day's wages (about $90 US today) and a talent of gold (probably about 120 pounds) was about 9,000 days' wages—a significant amount of money! Knowing this changes the way we view Jesus's parable of the talents (Matthew 25:14-30).

Time

Measuring time before clocks wasn't precise, but it was rather straightforward and easy to calculate.

Daytime

Sunrise—6 a.m.

First hour—7 a.m.

Second hour—8 a.m.

Third hour—9 a.m.

Fourth hour—10 a.m.

Fifth hour—11 a.m.

Sixth hour—Noon

Seventh hour—1 p.m.

Eighth hour—2 p.m.

Ninth hour—3 p.m.

Tenth hour—4 p.m.

Eleventh hour—5 p.m.

Sunset—6 p.m.

Nighttime

First watch—6 to 9 p.m.

Second watch—9 p.m. to midnight (Luke 12:38)

Third watch—Midnight to 3 a.m. (Luke 12:38)

Fourth watch—3 to 6 a.m. (Matthew 14:25)[4]

Geography

In the opening of Isaiah 9, the prophet writes, "In the past he humbled the land of Zebulun and the land of Naphtali, but in the future he will honor Galilee of the nations, by the Way of the Sea, beyond the Jordan."

Do you know where Zebulun and Naphtali are located? What about Galilee or the Jordan? Many of us see those geographic references and simply skim over them without knowing where they are located or why that might matter. Some might know this passage is a prophecy about where Jesus will set up the base of operations for his earthly ministry (Matthew 4:12-17), but even that doesn't help too much if you have to ask, "Where exactly is Capernaum?"

We don't need to become experts on biblical geography. But if children are completely unfamiliar with the geography of the Bible, it can impede their understanding of Scripture. With a mental map of where cities and countries mentioned are located, they can better grasp some of the essential elements of the biblical narrative.

We can close this knowledge gap and develop our mental model of the Bible by learning the basics of the historical geography. Geography has numerous facets we should know (such as the amount of rainfall) and methods for developing cartographic knowledge we should acquire. But for now, let's get started with these three tools for equipping your children.

1. *Choose reference markers.* You don't need to learn the location of every mountain, river, and town to build a mental model of biblical geography. A few key reference markers are often sufficient to quickly improve your understanding. For example, since Jesus often traveled to and from Capernaum, knowing the city's location can broaden your geographic frame of reference.

2. *Ask, "How far is that?"* Using a Bible atlas or online resource, you can quickly find the distance between any points in the Bible. For instance, when Jesus traveled from Nazareth to Capernaum, he traveled 30 miles—at least ten hours on foot.

3. *Draw to learn.* By making a hand-drawn map, your children can get a better grasp of geographic elements' relationship. Have them sketch out the boundaries (don't worry about it not being perfect), and then have them label five to ten reference points from memory (such as the Red Sea, Jerusalem, and the Jordan River). Compare their drawing to a Bible map and help them correct their errors. Have them frequently practice making such drawings, adding more reference points each time.

How to Read the Bible (Advanced)

Research has shown the biggest factor predicting the spiritual health of young adults is whether they read the Bible regularly as children. On average, children who frequently engaged in Bible reading had 12.5 percent higher "spiritual health" than otherwise comparable individuals who didn't, according to LifeWay Research. "The key takeaway from the study is a simple yet profound finding that God's Word truly is what changes lives," says Jana Magruder, director of LifeWay Kids.[1]

Because of the importance of regular engagement with Scripture, reading the Bible is one of the most important skills you can pass on to your children. By applying the techniques in the previous stages when they are younger, you should be able to lay a solid foundation. They'll refine and enhance their previously acquired skills as they get older and transition into the advanced literacy stage of Bible reading.

Don't be misled into thinking the advanced stage is reserved for pastors or Bible scholars. The advanced stage is merely the continuous development of our ability to read and comprehend the Bible. It's a lifelong process of improvement, not an end goal. With some effort, every believer who is functionally literate and open to learning new skills can become a better reader of the Bible. Just as you are a more skilled reader as an adult than you were as a child, your child will become a better reader over their lifetime by applying a few basic techniques.

The Golden Rule of Bible Reading

The *reason* we read the Bible is to hear God speak to us through the works of writers whom he inspired. Therefore our *goal* in Bible reading is to understand the meaning of what they wrote so we can more clearly grasp the message God wants us to hear, and so we may better know Jesus.

We should never respond to the Scripture by saying, "What this means to me is…" but instead should look for the meaning the author intended. As John Piper says,

> We might call it the Golden Rule of Bible Reading: do unto the biblical authors as you would have them do unto you. Our goal in Bible reading is not always easy to achieve, but it is straightforward. What did the author of this verse—or this chapter, or book—intend to communicate to his audience?[2]

If we follow this rule we will be motivated to acquire the skills necessary to understand the biblical authors' intended meaning. And if we don't follow this rule, we are merely wasting our time reading the Bible, for we will only hear an echo of our own minds rather than hear the mind of God.

Begin with an Overview of the Bible

Too often we treat the Bible as we would any other book—we think we must start at the beginning and read to the end. More specifically, we treat the Bible as two books, the Old Testament and its "sequel," the New Testament. But in fact, the Bible is a library of 66 books of various genres. That's why understanding what the Bible is all about can be difficult if we try to read it cover to cover.

If you or your child have never read the entire Bible before, R.C. Sproul recommends starting with this pattern, which includes a little more than one-third of all the books in Scripture.

Old Testament Overview

- Genesis (the history of creation, the fall, and God's covenantal dealings with the patriarchs)
- Exodus (the history of Israel's liberation and formation as a nation)
- Joshua (the history of the military conquest of the Promised Land)
- Judges (Israel's transition from a tribal federation to a monarchy)

- 1 Samuel (Israel's emerging monarchy under Saul and David)
- 2 Samuel (David's reign)
- 1 Kings (Solomon and the divided kingdom)
- 2 Kings (the fall of Israel)
- Ezra (the Israelites' return from exile)
- Nehemiah (the restoration of Jerusalem)
- Amos and Hosea (examples of minor prophets)
- Jeremiah (an example of a major prophet)
- Ecclesiastes (wisdom literature)
- Psalms and Proverbs (Hebrew poetry)

New Testament Overview

- The Gospel of Luke (the life of Jesus)
- Acts (the early church)
- Ephesians (an introduction to the teaching of Paul)
- 1 Corinthians (life in the church)
- 1 Peter (an introduction to Peter)
- 1 Timothy (an introduction to the Pastoral Epistles)
- Hebrews (Christology)
- Romans (Paul's theology)

"By reading these books, a student can get a basic feel for and understanding of the scope of the Bible without getting bogged down in the more difficult sections," says Sproul. "From there, he or she can fill in the gaps to complete the reading of the entire Bible."[3]

Recognize Biblical Genres

You wouldn't read a mortgage contract the way you would a novel, or read a poem like a church directory. You apply some of the same basic skills in reading all those formats, but understanding their meaning requires you to understand their genres. The same is true when reading the Bible.

A genre is simply an agreed upon conventional form of communication in a particular culture or group of cultures.[4] The use of genre provides clues to readers within a culture about how they should read a text. Those outside that culture, however, may not recognize the cues that would be familiar to someone inside the culture. Ancient Israelites, for example, would not understand "Once upon a time…" the same way we would, because they would not be familiar with the genre of fairy tales.

Similarly, we are often unaccustomed to the forms and conventions that were taken for granted by the authors who composed the Bible. To understand the author's meaning, we must be able to identify genres and recognize their characteristics.[5] Here are a few primary genres in the Bible.

- *Apocalyptic*—dramatic descriptions of a vision as seen by God's prophet. Examples are Daniel 7–12 and the book of Revelation.

- *Epistle*—a letter to a person or church. Examples are the book of James, 1 and 2 Peter, and the 13 letters of Paul to the Romans, Galatians, Ephesians, and so on.

- *Genealogy*—a list of names that define familial connections. The Bible contains about 25 genealogical lists, such as in 1 Chronicles 9 and Matthew 1:1-17.

- *Gospel*—similar to biographies but focused on the good news about Jesus. The four gospels are Matthew, Mark, Luke, and John.

- *Mosaic law*—instructions given by God to the Israelites found in the books of Exodus, Leviticus, Numbers, and Deuteronomy.

- *Parable*—a short story with a moral. The Gospels often portray Jesus teaching with parables.

- *Poetry*—verses that use symbolic and emotional language and imagery. Hebrew poetry doesn't rhyme but often uses parallelism. The most prominent example is the Psalms.

- *Prophecy*—messages from God regarding his will or the future.

Prophecies often use poetic language and imagery. Examples of prophecy are Isaiah and Amos.

- *Proverbial wisdom*—short sayings that provide practical advice on living. May be prose or, as in the case of the book of Proverbs, poetry.

Whenever you stumble across a passage that seems particularly difficult to understand, ask yourself two questions: (1) What type of genre or subgenre is this passage? (2) Do I understand the nuances of this genre?

An abundance of excellent books and online resources are available to help you better understand the genres found in the Bible. By studying them you can exponentially increase your appreciation and understanding of God's text.

Pray for God's Guidance

We read Scripture to know the mind of God. But if we are believers, we do not read it alone. We have the indwelling Holy Spirit to guide our understanding of God's Word. Just as the Spirit provided help by inspiring the original biblical authors, the Spirit will help us by illuminating Scripture so we can see the intended meaning of the text. Make a regular habit of praying the words of the psalmist: "Open my eyes that I may see wonderful things in your [teaching]" (Psalm 119:18).

Read the Bible

We may profit from reading books (like this one) on how to improve our ability to read Scripture. But nothing can substitute for sustained and consistent reading of large swaths of the Bible over extended periods of time. Ultimately, the best way to become a better reader of the Bible is to read the Bible.

Tips for Training Children

Use a "Reader's Bible" for Bible Reading

Bible reading differs from Bible study in pacing and focus (see chapter 6, "How to Study the Bible"). When we read the Bible, we tend to do so rapidly. Unfortunately, most modern Bible translations are designed for study, not reading. They often include supplementary material that can distract us from the

Scripture itself. And at a minimum, they include verse and chapter numbers that can impose an artificial organization on the text.

One way to overcome these potential stumbling blocks is to use the newly available *Readers Bible* (English Standard Version) or *The Books of the Bible* (New International Version). These format the text in a way that makes it more readable. For example, they often use a single-column text setting, a font optimized for reading, no cross-references or commentary, and a book-like format. Resources like these can be especially useful in helping your child read entire books of the Bible.

Teach Them How to Summarize Scripture

Dozens of biblical passages provide summaries, or theologically informed overviews, of previous sections of Scripture. Stephen's speech to the Sanhedrin in Acts 7 and Paul's speech at Pisidian Antioch in Acts 13:13-41 are good examples. These summaries show us how the Bible interprets itself. We can also create and use summaries to help our children become better students of God's Word.

Your child doesn't need a theologically detailed summary to get started. Start with simple summaries, such as "Leviticus: About the ceremonial law" or "Proverbs: The wise sayings of Solomon." As they gain a deeper understanding, they can modify the summaries. To help you get an idea of what they can look like, here are a few examples from some biblical scholars.[6]

- *Genesis*: The Creator God is faithful to his covenant promises and redeems humanity through the promised line, despite their sin and rebellion (Seulgi Byun).

- *Leviticus*: The holy God makes his people holy, calls them to be holy, and provides atonement through blood when they are not (Robin Weekes).

- *Joshua*: God gave the land he promised, and Israel took it (Liam Goligher).

Raise Your Expectations

Many of us who were raised as Christians struggle in our Bible reading because we were never taught to be serious students of the Bible. Our teachers and parents expected us to read lengthy novels for English class and learn the complicated vocabulary of biology and chemistry, but we weren't expected to take our Bible reading as seriously. Rarely were we expected to learn theological terms or read more than a chapter a day of Scripture.

Raise the bar for your own children. Have them devote the same level of effort to their Bible reading as they do for school activities. As Jen Wilkin notes,

> When the church says, "We know you're busy. Just invest a little time in the Bible," students understandably infer Christian discipleship falls below their other commitments. Since it requires so little of them, it must not be that important.
>
> What if we gave students the Bible and expected them to learn it? What if we asked them to read it like a book—to apply the same skills they are learning in their English class to their sacred text? Read entire books from start to finish. Annotate major themes. Summarize. Outline. Read repetitively.
>
> What if we asked them to learn to rightly divide the Word with all the discipline they would apply to learning calculus or the violin or gymnastics? In an age where the pattern for discipling students has been to repeatedly lower the bar, we should do what the soccer coach, the chemistry teacher, and the SAT prep instructor do: Raise it.[7]

How to See Jesus in the Old Testament

earning to see Jesus in all of Scripture helps us read the Bible as God intended—with Jesus as the primary subject. In John 5:39, Jesus says, "You study the Scriptures diligently because you think that in them you have eternal life. These are the very Scriptures that testify about me." Also, after his resurrection, Jesus joined two disciples on the road to Emmaus. "Beginning with Moses and all the Prophets, he explained to them what was said in all the Scriptures concerning himself" (Luke 24:27). Learning to see Jesus in the Old Testament helps us know him better.

Do you find reading the Old Testament boring? If so, you're not alone. Many Christians do—and many of them are afraid to admit it. Parents may even worry that encouraging their children to read the early books of Scripture will cause them to lose interest in reading the Bible altogether. We can change this by learning to see Jesus throughout Scripture.

Numerous tools can be used to learn to see Jesus in the Old Testament, but we'll limit our focus to one of the most common and useful: typology.

Seeing Jesus Through Typology

Biblical typology affirms that God works in recurring patterns throughout history. A type is an event or person that prefigures a future event or person (the antitype).[1] Not all typology in the Bible is about Jesus (see for example Galatians 4:25–27), but more Old Testament typology points to him than to any other person or thing.

In biblical interpretation, a type of Christ is a real person, place, object, event, or office God has ordained to act as a predictive pattern or resemblance of Jesus's person and work, or as an opposition to both.[2] An antitype is the object or person corresponding to or foreshadowed in a type. For example, in Matthew 12:42, Jesus says he's a greater Solomon. King Solomon is the type and Jesus is the antitype. (For our purposes in this entry, the term "antitype" will always refer to Jesus.)

But wait…isn't this a type of allegorical reading of Scripture that can lead to heretical interpretations? No, because an allegory is a story, poem, or picture that can be interpreted to reveal a hidden meaning, typically a moral, religious, or political one. The key differences between allegory and typology are that an allegory can be fictional and is open to a range of interpretative possibilities, while typology is real and factual and its interpretation must be consistent with the true and literal meaning of the original text. Allegorical interpretation of Scripture should be avoided.[3]

How do we find types of Jesus? Begin by reconsidering the tales of Bible heroes, seeing them as types of Jesus. Many of us were taught that Bible stories were moral lessons we can apply to our own lives. For example, the tale of David and Goliath (1 Samuel 17) is taken as a lesson that we, the underdogs (we always see ourselves as David, never Goliath), can succeed if only we have faith and courage.

But we aren't David, for David is a type of Jesus. The shepherd boy is God's chosen mediator who is victorious over the implacable foe, just as Jesus wins the victory over sin and death. We don't fully understand the story until we realize it's not a heroic tale for us to emulate but a foreshadowing of the work of Christ.

Tips for Training Children

Becoming Old Testament Cryptographers

Since at least the time of ancient Egypt, humans have passed on important and secret information using cryptography. In fact, the term "cryptography" comes from the Greek words *kryptos* and *graphein*, which mean "hidden" and "writing." The earliest form of cryptography was the simple writing of a message that could not be understood by most people unless they had a special "key" that allowed them to unlock the meaning.

Many children are naturally interested in cryptography—sending and receiving messages using code or ciphers and discovering hidden messages. This can be a key way to interest them in the Old Testament, since these writings are, in a sense, the most important work of cryptography ever produced. Explain to them the Old Testament is like a secret code that cannot be fully understood unless they have the special key that unlocks its hidden meanings. The special key is Jesus.[4]

Have them read the "code" (a Bible passage or story) and try to identify the ways the passage speaks about Jesus.

Start with Animals

A helpful way for younger children to see Jesus in the Old Testament is to look for the animals. Animals or references to animals in Scripture are frequently types of Jesus. Children should especially look for lambs, since they are the most important animals in the Bible. As Nancy Guthrie says, all the lambs in the Old Testament point us toward one very special Lamb, "the Lamb of God" (John 1:29). "I don't think it would be an overstatement to say that if we do not grasp the story of the Lamb," adds Guthrie, "we cannot grasp the story of the Bible."[5]

Encourage Them to Be Bold

You may be concerned children will start seeing types that aren't there, as Joe Rigney explains.

> For many evangelicals, such typological interpretation is fraught with danger. A host of questions immediately arises: Are we justified in seeing Christ in the Old Testament only in those places explicitly mentioned by the biblical authors? Or can we imitate apostolic interpretive methods and find Jesus in other places in Scripture?[6]

Rigney notes that Jonathan Edwards, one of the greatest Christian minds in American history, believed the entire Old Testament gives us a "typical (or typological) world." To Edwards, everything in the Old Testament is typological, and so he believed it is unreasonable to restrict types to the explicitly interpreted instances in Scripture. "For by Scripture it is plain that innumerable other things are types that are not interpreted in Scripture (all the ordinances of the law are all shadows of good things to come)."

Encourage your children to be bold in using Scripture to find ways it might reveal Jesus to them.

How to Study the Bible

B ible *study* is not the same thing as Bible *reading*," says David Mathis. "If Bible reading is like raking for leaves, Bible study is like digging for diamonds. The Christian life calls for both."[1]

Two key differences between reading and study are pacing and focus. When we read the Bible, we generally do so at the quickest pace our comprehension will allow. We may consume large chunks at one time, such as reading an entire book. We also look for the broad outlines of the text to know what it's about or to determine how it fits into the larger scope of God's Word. Bible reading precedes Bible study because it provides the broad perspective we need before we narrow in on specific passages.

When we study the Bible, we slow down to focus on the meaning of the text. We read and reread shorter units of text and spend more time focusing on specific words, clauses, verses, and paragraphs. We also ask questions of the text: What does this word mean? Why did the author use this unique phrase? How does this apply to my own life?

The essence of Bible study is asking questions of the text to discover the meaning God intended.

Of the many profitable ways to study the Bible, one that everyone from preteens to Old Testament scholars has found to be particularly helpful is the inductive Bible study method. The inductive study method is an investigative approach to the Bible using three basic components:

- Observation: What does the text say?

- Interpretation: What does the text mean?
- Application: How does the meaning of the text apply to life?[2]

How to Observe a Text

In other entries we will drill down into interpretation and application of Scripture (see chapters 7 and 8, "How to Interpret the Bible" and "How to Apply Scripture to Your Life"). But for now, we'll focus on the observation component.

Ask Basic Questions

Begin by asking the basic questions to orient yourself to the text you will study. For example, who wrote it? What is the genre (letter, narrative, history…)? When was it written? Where was the author when it was written? Why did the author write this letter?

Words, Phrases, and Relationships Between Prepositions

Ask about what the author meant by using specific words and phrases. Don't assume your definition or understanding of terms is the same as the author's. Look for words that are repeated or given special emphasis, and pay special attention to connecting words ("but," "if," "and," "therefore," "in order that," "because"…). "Sometimes the major differences between whole theologies hang on these connections," says John Piper.[3]

Make Lists

In 2 Peter 1:5-9, we find a list of virtues we should combine:

> For this very reason, make every effort to add to your faith goodness; and to goodness, knowledge; and to knowledge, self-control; and to self-control, perseverance; and to perseverance, godliness; and to godliness, mutual affection; and to mutual affection, love. For if you possess these qualities in increasing measure, they will keep you from being ineffective and unproductive in your knowledge of our Lord Jesus Christ. But whoever does not have them is nearsighted and blind, forgetting that they have been cleansed from their past sins.

When we read this passage, we can easily jumble the virtues together. To keep them straight so you can reflect on them more carefully, put them in a list:

1. Faith

2. Goodness

3. Knowledge

4. Self-control

5. Perseverance

6. Godliness

7. Mutual affection

8. Love

Using lists in our note-taking can help us track key words, phrases, and concepts.

Contrasts and Comparisons

Contrasts and comparisons are used throughout the Bible to focus our attention. Consider in the passage cited above how Peter compares people who possess those virtues (they are effective and productive) with those who don't (they are nearsighted and blind).

Metaphors

When we come across metaphors in our study, we should stop and use our imagination to think through the meaning. For instance, how would lacking perseverance be similar to being nearsighted?

Expressions of Time and Terms of Conclusion

Be on the lookout for words that mark expression of time, such as "before," "after," "during," "since," "for," "already," and so on. These terms can help you see the sequence or timing of events and lead to a more accurate interpretation of Scripture.[4] Similarly, terms of conclusion, such as "therefore," "thus," and "for this reason," point to an ending or a summary.[5]

Connections to Other Parts of the Bible

Search for connections to other parts of Scripture. For example, where can the virtues on Peter's list be found in other passages? What do other biblical authors say about the importance of those virtues?

Question to Improve Your Observation Skills

These are just a few of the ways you can engage the text during the observation phase of study. Look for other ways by carefully considering the questions that arise in your study and asking yourself, "What type of question am I asking?" When you identify a broader category, give it a name you will remember and use in the future. For example, if you find yourself asking, "What emotional response is the author expecting to evoke?" you could use that to consider other questions about affections and emotions. Give it a label like "Affective Questions" and add it as a tool in your Bible study tool kit.

Tips for Training Children

Incorporate Prayer

Bible study is about looking for God's meaning in his Word, so we need to constantly be talking to him, asking him to reveal his meaning to us. Next to the Bible itself, prayer is our most important tool for Bible study. Build a strong foundation in your child by encouraging them to be praying before, during, and after their study efforts.

A Special Bible for Studying

Teach your child that to show reverence to God's Word often entails messing up the pages. We need to scribble notes, underline passages, and mark key words and phrases. Give them their own Bible they can mark up. Wide-margin and journaling Bibles are ideal, though just about any Bible you have around will serve the purpose.

A Life of Study

Studying the Bible is difficult work that requires focus and attention—two traits children often lack. Be patient with them and don't expect too much over a brief time. If you pile on too much work for each study session, the child will get the impression Bible study is drudgery. Prepare them for the challenges of concerted study, but don't expect them to suddenly become Bible scholars. Keep your expectations realistic and modest, and keep the long-term goal in focus—training your child to be a lifelong student of the Bible.

7

How to Interpret the Bible

Of the three steps of Bible study—observation, interpretation, and application—the middle one is often the most daunting. We may hear words like "hermeneutics" (the science of interpretation) or "exegesis" (critical explanation or interpretation of a text) and think interpretation is something best left to experts.

While we should certainly take advantage of the expertise of pastors, scholars, and theologians, basic interpretation of the Bible is a necessary task for every believer. Here are five principles that should guide your efforts as you learn to interpret the Bible.

Don't Go It Alone

Never has the average person living in a Western country had access to such an abundance of superb biblical scholarship as we do today. Many excellent and inexpensive concordances, commentaries, and study Bibles are available, as well as a vast array of free online resources. Let these tools help you understand and interpret what God is saying in his Word. The Bible is a gift given to the church, so we should join with our brothers and sisters (including through books and other resources) in searching for its meaning.

Context Is Key

Noting the various contexts—historical, social, political, and so on—will help us understand and interpret a text, but we should pay special attention to the literary context. Look at the verses, paragraphs, and chapters immediately before and after a passage to understand what the writer intended. "The writers of the Bible included enough within each book of the Bible to help the readers understand that book of the Bible without referring to information they lacked," says New Testament scholar Craig Keener. "For that reason, context is the most important academic key to Bible interpretation."[1]

The Plain and Obvious Meaning

A passage may be difficult to understand because its context is unfamiliar to us. But we should always assume the meaning is straightforward and would have been understood by the Bible author's contemporaries. "A common and persistent myth about the Bible is that its real meaning is hidden behind the surface message," says Wayne McDill. "Even though the Bible uses symbolic or figurative language, most of it is clear to the reader. Even when you do not know about the people, places, and events in question, you can grasp the point of the text."[2]

The Bible Interprets the Bible

All Scripture is inspired by God (2 Timothy 3:16), so no part of the Bible contradicts the other parts. Use the clearer texts to shed light on passages that are harder to understand. And because God's revelation is cumulative, use the parts that came later to understand what came before. For example, use the New Testament to interpret the Old Testament.

The Singular Meaning

Each passage of the Bible has a single and specific meaning, which means it has a single and specific interpretation. This is an extremely important principle. A passage may have numerous *applications* or lessons we can learn from it, but it will have only one meaning and one interpretation. "Every text of Scripture has one true interpretation," says John MacArthur. "We might not get them all right, we might disagree, but all texts of Scripture have one interpretation, one only. That is the essence of communication. God is saying something, not anything you want Him to say, and not everything."[3]

Tips for Training Children

Three Questions for Interpretation

Here is a simple model for teaching children how to interpret the Bible. Have them ask these three questions:

1. What does this passage teach me about God?
2. What does this passage teach me about human beings (or myself)?
3. What does this passage teach me about the need for and the coming of a Savior?

"Often the first two questions answer the third," says Sara Wallace. "Why not sit down with your kids and try this approach together? Pick a passage of Scripture and ask these three questions."[4]

Work Around Their Interest

As we've discussed before, the purpose of Bible study is not to turn your child into a pint-sized scholar, but to instill in them a lifelong love for learning Scripture. Asking kids to grind out interpretations of Isaiah or Nahum before they are ready could be counterproductive.

All 66 books of the Bible are important, but they aren't equally interesting or relevant to your child. Because children have limited time for study (and limited interest in it), focus on the topics or passages that most interest them. Talk to them about which parts of the Bible to start with or focus on. Their motives for choosing a passage probably won't be purely noble, but trust God to use their interest for his own purposes.

Don't Rush Them to Application

Application is an essential aspect of Bible study. But too often we don't spend enough time doing the hard word of observation and interpretation because we want to get to the "relevant" part ("What does this mean for *me*?"). We need to ensure we are teaching our children that observing and interpreting God's Word is itself valuable and not just a process to be endured to get to the application stage.

8

How to Apply Scripture to Your Life

The apostle Paul says everything in the Bible was "written to teach us" (Romans 15:4). Because the Bible was written in various times and contexts, we are left with the challenge of figuring out how God's Word applies to us. Or as David Powlison says, "Your challenge is always to *reapply* Scripture afresh, because God's purpose is always to *rescript* your life."[1]

How do we go about the process of applying the Scripture to our own lives? Here are five general ways.

Direct Commands

The most obvious passages for personal application are those in which God gives direct commands. The Bible contains about a thousand commands, though many are repetitions or restatements of general requirements. For instance, some of the most frequently repeated commands in the Bible are "praise the Lord," "do not be afraid," "rejoice," and "give thanks," all of which, as Jon Bloom observes, are "commands, in essence, to be happy."[2]

General Truths

Scripture frequently provides general truths broadly applicable to a variety of situations and then leaves it to us to discern how they should be applied. In Matthew 22:21, Jesus says to give back to "Caesar what is Caesar's, and to God what is God's." Rather than giving us a list of what belongs to God and what is due the government, Jesus expects us to use godly wisdom to apply this general rule and work out the details for ourselves.

Indirect Analogy

Sometimes a passage teaches us by example rather than through a stated rule. This is the old-fashioned "Sunday school morality," in which we look to the Old Testament narratives to learn how we should or should not act. For example, in the story of the attempted seduction of Joseph by Potiphar's wife, we learn to flee from sexual sin and adultery (Genesis 39:7-12).

We must be careful, of course, not to think the personal application derived from such stories is the primary purpose of the narrative. Although Joseph's actions were a godly example, they resulted in his being thrown in prison— a situation God used to carry out his larger purposes. Whenever we apply the Bible indirectly, we need to keep in mind that the Bible is not about us, but about God.

The most important principle in using human examples from the Bible, especially from the Old Testament, is to follow what Scripture says to follow and avoid what Scripture says to avoid. Our first question when considering a human example is, what does the Bible say about them? For example, Paul refers to events in Exodus and Numbers and says, "These things occurred as examples to keep us from setting our hearts on evil things as they did" (1 Corinthians 10:6). Paul is clear that the Israelites are often examples of what *not* to do.

Indirect Extension

Most of Scripture is composed of neither direct commands nor generally applicable truths. For instance, consider the lists of names and genealogies found in the Old Testament. How do we apply those passages to our own lives? Powlison offers this guidance:

> In one sense, such passages apply exactly because they are *not* about you. Understood rightly, such passages give a changed perspective. They locate you on a bigger stage. They teach you to notice God and other people in their own right. They call you to understand yourself within a story—many stories—bigger than your personal history and immediate concerns. They locate you within a community far wider than your immediate network of relationships. And they remind you that you are always in God's presence, under his eye, and part of his program.[3]

The endurance and encouragement Paul refers to in Romans 15:4 come from reading the Old Testament and understanding we are part of God's story. We can see the promises God made to his people, see how he was always faithful, and be encouraged to endure, knowing he will likewise always be faithful to us.

Direct Analogy

Many contemporary controversies and concerns are not directly mentioned in the Bible. In some circumstances, we can personally apply biblical principles to situations similar to those mentioned in the Bible. One helpful way to appeal to Scripture on moral issues is to use analogical reasoning.[4]

When we use analogies, we compare parallel cases, transferring information or meaning from one subject (the source) to another (the target). For example, when Jesus says he is the bread of life (John 6:35), he is noting a characteristic of the source (the life-sustaining nature of bread) and applying it to a target (Jesus himself is life-sustaining). In analogical reasoning, we reason from like to like, not identical to identical.

James Gustafson says this about the commonly accepted method of scriptural analogy:

> Those actions of persons and groups are to be judged morally wrong which are similar to actions that are judged to be wrong or against God's will under similar circumstances in Scripture, or are discordant with actions judged to be right or in accord with God's will in Scripture.[5]

Although almost any part of the Bible can be used to reason analogically (such as narrative passages), the clearest path is to focus on scriptural commands, proverbs, and rules. These are easier to make a clear "like to like" comparison, allowing us to be reasonably certain we are applying biblical principles effectively.

Consider, for example, the proverbial claim in Hosea 4:11: "Old wine and new wine take away their understanding." This passage refers to drunkenness, which is always condemned in the Bible.[6] With analogical reasoning we understand that other substances that have an intoxicating effect and "take away our understanding" might also be sinful.

For example, we might ask whether it is sinful to use narcotics, such as heroin, for social or recreational purposes (as opposed to medicinal use). Many Christians would consider the answer to be rather straightforward, but this extreme example highlights the reasoning process that allows us to apply biblical principles to our personal life through direct analogy.

We can answer the question by noting the characteristics of narcotics and looking for similarities to a scriptural example. Legal scholar Cass Sunstein explains how we apply analogical reasoning:

> This kind of thinking has a simple structure: (1) A has characteristic X; (2) B shares that characteristic; (3) A also has characteristic Y; (4) Because A and B share characteristic X, we conclude what is not yet known, that B shares characteristic Y as well.[7]

If we apply analogical reasoning to our example, here's what we find:

> A (intoxication by alcohol ingestion) has characteristic X (produces a psychoactive effect—it affects brain function, resulting in alterations in perception, mood, consciousness, cognition, and behavior).
> B (intoxication by narcotics) shares that characteristic.
> Because A and B share characteristic X, we conclude what is not yet known, that B shares characteristic Y (is an action that is judged to be against God's will; that is, is sinful).

With analogical reasoning, we can determine that if narcotics are used recreationally to achieve some level of intoxication, the motive and action are clearly sinful.

Such reasoning is not foolproof, of course. We may misunderstand the intention or relevant aspects of a biblical command and misapply it to a new situation. Similarly, we may choose irrelevant aspects of comparison that can lead us to draw the wrong conclusions. Yet despite these concerns, analogical reasoning can be a powerful tool that helps us think more clearly and biblically about moral problems.

Tips for Training Children

Don't Start with Application

Many generations of children were brought up to believe in what Dallas Willard calls the "gospel of sin management," in which "the Christian message is thought to be essentially concerned only with how to deal with sin: with wrongdoing or wrong-being and its effects."[8] The Bible was taught in a manner that led children to believe its main purpose was to tell us how to behave properly rather than being primarily about Jesus.

In chapter 7, we noted three questions that help kids read the Bible through the lens of the gospel:

- What does this passage teach me about God?
- What does this passage teach me about human beings (or myself)?
- What does this passage teach me about the need for and the coming of a Savior?

"What about application?" asks Sara Wallace. "It's coming. But begin by laying the foundation. Once your kids develop a habit of seeing answers to these three questions, they'll then be able to ask, 'What does God want me to do?' We can only apply the Bible properly to our lives when the gospel is the driving force."[9]

Bible Heroes and the Jesus-Lens

When teaching your child to emulate a biblical hero using indirect analogy, do it indirectly. The child shouldn't learn, "I need to be like David," or "I need to be like Esther," but rather, "When he slew Goliath, David was like Jesus," or "When Esther showed courage, she was being like Jesus." As Tim Keller says, Jesus is the true and better Adam, the true and better David, the true and better Esther, and so on. We look to them as examples because they point to the "true and better" example.

With Commands, Start from the New Testament

When reading the Old Testament, it's not always easy to tell which direct commands apply to us today and which were meant for the Israelites. Therefore it's generally helpful to have children start with New Testament commands. Most that are still applicable can be found there anyway. For example, each of the Ten Commandments is explicitly confirmed in the New Testament.[10]

9

How to Meditate on God's Word

The concept of meditation can confuse and even frighten Bible-believing Christians—and rightly so. When we hear the word "meditate," we often think of people sitting cross-legged, chanting, "Omm," and reflecting on Zen koans, like "What is the sound of one hand clapping?" Those are often associated with transcendental meditation and other practices borrowed from Eastern religions that conflict with biblical spirituality.

"Many Eastern religions teach that the source of salvation is found within, and that the fundamental human problem is not sin against a holy God but ignorance of our true condition," notes philosopher Douglas Groothuis. "These worldviews advocate meditation and 'higher forms of consciousness' as a way to discover a secret inner divinity."[1]

But that's not the biblical meaning of meditation. Neither is it the idea we can visit nature to get in touch with God. Psalm 19:1 tell us that nature declares the glory of God. But as pastor John Starke says, "The point of Psalm 19 isn't that nature can perfectly reveal God to us, but that if we are going to look to nature to see God's glory, we better do so with our Bibles open!"[2]

So, what is biblical meditation? See if you notice a pattern, repeated throughout the Bible, found in Psalm 119:

- "I meditate on your precepts and consider your ways" (verse 15).
- "Oh, how I love your law! I meditate on it all day long" (verse 97).

Notice that the psalmist is meditating on God's works and words. How does meditating on Scripture differ from simply reading or studying the Bible? One key difference is that biblical meditation is listening to the truth in the presence of God. Meditation is a way of keeping our mind on God's Word even after our eyes have left the text of Scripture. When we meditate on Scripture, we keep our mind fixed on God's Word.

Here are three methods to help you and your children keep a focus on Scripture.

Ruminate on the Individual Words

The term "ruminate" describes the way some animals—such as cows, sheep, and giraffes—can bring up food from their stomach and chew again what has already been chewed and swallowed. Similarly, "ruminate" describes the mental process of bringing up thoughts to go over them again repeatedly in our mind, often casually or slowly.

We often gulp down God's Word without savoring it or fully extracting the nourishment it provides. Jean Fleming suggests an alternative:

> Instead, we need to chew the words [of Scripture], roll them around in our mouths, and suck the sweetness from them. This process is called meditation…The Lord calls us to the life of meditation and promises tremendous benefit to the "chewer."[3]

One way to "chew" on the text is to repeat a verse or phrase with emphasis on a different word each time. For example, this is how we might ruminate on a phrase in John 2:5 (spoken by Mary to some servants but applicable to us also):

> *Do* whatever he tells you.
>
> Do *whatever* he tells you.
>
> Do whatever *he* tells you.
>
> Do whatever he *tells* you.
>
> Do whatever he tells *you*.

By shifting the emphasis, we can more clearly see the various shades of meaning and deepen our understanding of the verse. This can become a fun game for younger children, helping them focus on Scripture in an entertaining way.

Ask the Philippians 4:8 Questions

When helping your child meditate on a scriptural event, experience, thing, or encounter, encourage them to ask these questions:

What is *true* about this, or what truth does it exemplify?

What is *honorable* about this?

What is *right* about this?

What is *pure* about this, or how does it exemplify purity?

What is *lovely* about this?

What is *admirable, commendable,* or *reputation-strengthening* about this?

What is *excellent* about this (how does it excel others of this kind)?

What is *praiseworthy* about this?

Ask the Joseph Hall Questions

In his book *The Art of Divine Meditation*, written in 1606, the English Puritan Joseph Hall lists several questions to ask of a Scripture passage for meditation.[4]

What is it? (Define and/or describe what it is.)

What are its divisions or parts?

What causes it?

What does it cause (what are its fruits and effects)?

What is its place, location, or use?

What are its qualities and attachments?

What is contrary or contradictory to it? What is different from it?

What compares to it?

What are its titles or names?

What are the testimonies or examples of Scripture about it?

These questions can tell you a lot about how much a child is getting out of their Scripture meditation exercises.

10

How to Memorize Bible Verses

In other chapters of this book we discuss ways to memorize everything from lists to entire biblical narratives. Unfortunately, those methods aren't particularly helpful when trying to learn text—like Bible verses—with word-for-word precision. Memorizing text verbatim requires an application of time and repetition that is simple but a bit exhausting.

These steps to memorize Bible verses or brief passages work for adults and for children.

Look and Speak

Have the child focus their eyes intently on the words of the verse as they read the passage out loud five to twenty times.

Speak and Write

After reading the words, have the child attempt to write or type the verses as they say them aloud. If they forget a word, have them go back and use the "look and speak" method three times before making another attempt to write the verse. Have them speak and write the verse five to twenty times during each memorization session.

Repeat and Refresh

Once they can recite the verse from memory, have them repeat it to you three times a day for the next several days. Then have them repeat—or pray—the words once a day for a month.

11

How to Memorize Entire Books of the Bible

Now that your child can memorize individual verses, it's time for a substantial challenge—memorizing an entire book of the Bible.

If they can memorize verses, they can memorize a book. All it takes is time, effort, and perseverance. Here are a few tips for building this habit.

Make It Doable and Rewarding

Memorizing an entire book of the Bible is a challenge for anyone, but by applying a few tips we can make it less daunting.

First, unless you have a strong preference for a certain Bible translation, choose a version that is easy to learn. This is likely to be a phrase-for-phrase (dynamic equivalent) translation, like the New International Version.

Second, start with a book that is neither too long nor too short—between 100 and 160 verses. Consider Philippians (104 verses), 1 Peter (105 verses), James (108 verses), Galatians (149 verses), or Ephesians (155 verses).

Finally, offer a suitable reward for achieving the goal. Over time your child will learn why memorizing Bible books is personally enriching. But when building this habit, a more tangible reward can provide a strong incentive to persevere.

Learn a Verse a Day

Each day have the child read the verse out loud to you ten times. They'll be tempted to look up from time to time to see what they've retained, but encourage them to focus intently on the words as if they were taking a mental picture of the text.

Consider Memorizing the Verse Numbers

If the child finds this exercise exceedingly difficult, consider having them memorize the verse numbers too. For example, if they're memorizing 1 Peter 1:3-5, they'd say, "(One-three) Praise be to the God and Father of our Lord Jesus Christ! In his great mercy he has given us new birth into a living hope through the resurrection of Jesus Christ from the dead, (one-four) and into an inheritance that can never perish, spoil or fade. This inheritance is kept in heaven for you, (one-five) who through faith are shielded by God's power until the coming of the salvation that is ready to be revealed in the last time."

Memorizing the verse numbers as if they were part of each verse can help prevent them from dropping out verses or even whole paragraphs later.[1]

Review Previous Verses

Each day, before attempting to learn new verses, have them review the previous verses they've memorized by reciting them for you. Start by having them say the verses from the day before out loud ten times as they try to picture the words in their mind. Then have them recite *all* the previous verses from the beginning of the book. If they get stuck, tell them the next few words or have them look at their Bible. Don't skip this step: Repetition and visualization are the keys to effective memorization. Only after they've completed this step should they work on learning new verses.

Retain What They've Memorized...

After they've learned an entire book, have them recite every verse—from beginning to end—every day for 90 consecutive days. Thereafter, have them try to recite the book at least once a week indefinitely.

...But Don't Be Upset When They Forget

The unfortunate reality is that over time they'll forget most of what they've memorized. This happens even to Christians who have spent years memorizing

Scripture—and it will happen to your child too. Yet the effort they put into learning the verses will pay off later in their Bible studies. Having once internalized entire books of God's Word, they'll be able to interact more meaningfully with his text.

12

How to Read the Entire Bible

To develop a biblical worldview, we need to saturate our minds with Scripture. This requires repeatedly reading and engaging with the Bible throughout our lifetime. The earlier we begin reading the Bible, the more time we have for God's Word to seep into the marrow of our souls. That's why helping a child develop the habit of Bible reading is one of the greatest gifts we can give them.

Numerous Bible reading plans are available that can help older children read through Scripture in a year. But as many adults who have begun such plans on New Year's Day can attest, they are difficult to follow consistently and are usually abandoned by Valentine's Day. We miss a few days, try to catch up, and eventually give up out of frustration. Here's a simpler approach that is ideal for children.

Make a Chart—or Use Mine

Turn to the chart at the end of this chapter. In the left column, you'll see every book of the Bible, and in the right column, you'll see a number for every chapter in each book.[1]

Your child might enjoy using the chart as a template and making their own.

Read a Chapter a Day

Read a chapter from a different genre of Scripture each day. Here's a pattern you can follow.

Sunday: poetry

Monday: Pentateuch

Tuesday: Old Testament history, part 1

Wednesday: Old Testament history, part 2

Thursday: Old Testament prophets

Friday: New Testament history

Saturday: New Testament letters[2]

You may want to modify this plan for younger children, leaving out some sections (such as the Old Testament prophets) until they are older.

Record Your Progress

After the child reads each chapter, have them check it off on the chart. When they complete an entire book, highlight it so it stands out on the page. Marking off the chapters will give them a sense of accomplishment.

And that's the plan—it's that simple. If they miss a day, just have them move on to the next section. If it takes longer than two and a half years, don't sweat it—there's no rush. Be persistent but easygoing, encouraging rather than demanding. The goal is to help your child develop a desire to read the Bible and a habit of doing it. Even if the child can't complete the entire reading program in a year, if they follow the plan regularly they'll have read large sections of Scripture.

THE OLD TESTAMENT	
The Pentateuch	
Genesis	1 2 3 4 5 6 7 8 9 10 11 12 13 14 15 16 17 18 19 20 21 22 23 24 25 26 27 28 29 30 31 32 33 34 35 36 37 38 39 40 41 42 43 44 45 46 47 48 49 50
Exodus	1 2 3 4 5 6 7 8 9 10 11 12 13 14 15 16 17 18 19 20 21 22 23 24 25 26 27 28 29 30 31 32 33 34 35 36 37 38 39 40
Leviticus	1 2 3 4 5 6 7 8 9 10 11 12 13 14 15 16 17 18 19 20 21 22 23 24 25 26 27
Numbers	1 2 3 4 5 6 7 8 9 10 11 12 13 14 15 16 17 18 19 20 21 22 23 24 25 26 27 28 29 30 31 32 33 34 35 36
Deuteronomy	1 2 3 4 5 6 7 8 9 10 11 12 13 14 15 16 17 18 19 20 21 22 23 24 25 26 27 28 29 30 31 32 33 34
Old Testament History part 1	

Joshua	1 2 3 4 5 6 7 8 9 10 11 12 13 14 15 16 17 18 19 20 21 22 23 24
Judges	1 2 3 4 5 6 7 8 9 10 11 12 13 14 15 16 17 18 19 20 21
Ruth	1 2 3 4
1 Samuel	1 2 3 4 5 6 7 8 9 10 11 12 13 14 15 16 17 18 19 20 21 22 23 24 25 26 27 28 29 30 31
2 Samuel	1 2 3 4 5 6 7 8 9 10 11 12 13 14 15 16 17 18 19 20 21 22 23 24
1 Kings	1 2 3 4 5 6 7 8 9 10 11 12 13 14 15 16 17 18 19 20 21 22
2 Kings	1 2 3 4 5 6 7 8 9 10 11 12 13 14 15 16 17 18 19 20 21 22 23 24 25
Old Testament History part 2	
1 Chronicles	1 2 3 4 5 6 7 8 9 10 11 12 13 14 15 16 17 18 19 20 21 22 23 24 25 26 27 28 29
2 Chronicles	1 2 3 4 5 6 7 8 9 10 11 12 13 14 15 16 17 18 19 20 21 22 23 24 25 26 27 28 29 30 31 32 33 34 35 36
Ezra	1 2 3 4 5 6 7 8 9 10
Nehemiah	1 2 3 4 5 6 7 8 9 10 11 12 13
Esther	1 2 3 4 5 6 7 8 9 10
Job	1 2 3 4 5 6 7 8 9 10 11 12 13 14 15 16 17 18 19 20 21 22 23 24 25 26 27 28 29 30 31 32 33 34 35 36 37 38 39 40 41 42
Old Testament Poetry	
Psalms	1 2 3 4 5 6 7 8 9 10 11 12 13 14 15 16 17 18 19 20 21 22 23 24 25 26 27 28 29 30 31 32 33 34 35 36 37 38 39 40 41 42 43 44 45 46 47 48 49 50 51 52 53 54 55 56 57 58 59 60 61 62 63 64 65 66 67 68 69 70 71 72 73 74 75 76 77 78 79 80 81 82 83 84 85 86 87 88 89 90 91 92 93 94 95 96 97 98 99 100 101 102 103 104 105 106 107 108 109 110 111 112 113 114 115 116 117 118 119 120 121 122 123 124 125 126 127 128 129 130 131 132 133 134 135 136 137 138 139 140 141 142 143 144 145 146 147 148 149 150
Proverbs	1 2 3 4 5 6 7 8 9 10 11 12 13 14 15 16 17 18 19 20 21 22 23 24 25 26 27 28 29 30 31
Ecclesiastes	1 2 3 4 5 6 7 8 9 10 11 12
Song of Solomon	1 2 3 4 5 6 7 8

Old Testament Prophets	
Isaiah	1 2 3 4 5 6 7 8 9 10 11 12 13 14 15 16 17 18 19 20 21 22 23 24 25 26 27 28 29 30 31 32 33 34 35 36 37 38 39 40 41 42 43 44 45 46 47 48 49 50 51 52 53 54 55 56 57 58 59 60 61 62 63 64 65 66
Jeremiah	1 2 3 4 5 6 7 8 9 10 11 12 13 14 15 16 17 18 19 20 21 22 23 24 25 26 27 28 29 30 31 32 33 34 35 36 37 38 39 40 41 42 43 44 45 46 47 48 49 50 51 52
Lamentations	1 2 3 4 5
Ezekiel	1 2 3 4 5 6 7 8 9 10 11 12 13 14 15 16 17 18 19 20 21 22 23 24 25 26 27 28 29 30 31 32 33 34 35 36 37 38 39 40 41 42 43 44 45 46 47 48
Daniel	1 2 3 4 5 6 7 8 9 10 11 12
Hosea	1 2 3 4 5 6 7 8 9 10 11 12 13 14
Joel	1 2 3
Amos	1 2 3 4 5 6 7 8 9
Obadiah	1
Jonah	1 2 3 4
Micah	1 2 3 4 5 6 7
Nahum	1 2 3
Habakkuk	1 2 3
Zephaniah	1 2 3
Haggai	1 2
Zechariah	1 2 3 4 5 6 7 8 9 10 11 12 13 14
Malachi	1 2 3 4
THE NEW TESTAMENT	
New Testament History	
Matthew	1 2 3 4 5 6 7 8 9 10 11 12 13 14 15 16 17 18 19 20 21 22 23 24 25 26 27 28
Mark	1 2 3 4 5 6 7 8 9 10 11 12 13 14 15 16
Luke	1 2 3 4 5 6 7 8 9 10 11 12 13 14 15 16 17 18 19 20 21 22 23 24
John	1 2 3 4 5 6 7 8 9 10 11 12 13 14 15 16 17 18 19 20 21
Acts	1 2 3 4 5 6 7 8 9 10 11 12 13 14 15 16 17 18 19 20 21 22 23 24 25 26 27 28

New Testament Letters	
Romans	1 2 3 4 5 6 7 8 9 10 11 12 13 14 15 16
1 Corinthians	1 2 3 4 5 6 7 8 9 10 11 12 13 14 15 16
2 Corinthians	1 2 3 4 5 6 7 8 9 10 11 12 13
Galatians	1 2 3 4 5 6
Ephesians	1 2 3 4 5 6
Philippians	1 2 3 4
Colossians	1 2 3 4
1 Thessalonians	1 2 3 4 5
2 Thessalonians	1 2 3
1 Timothy	1 2 3 4 5 6
2 Timothy	1 2 3 4
Titus	1 2 3
Philemon	1
Hebrews	1 2 3 4 5 6 7 8 9 10 11 12 13
James	1 2 3 4 5
1 Peter	1 2 3 4 5
2 Peter	1 2 3
1 John	1 2 3 4 5
2 John	1
3 John	1
Jude	1
Revelation	1 2 3 4 5 6 7 8 9 10 11 12 13 14 15 16 17 18 19 20 21 22

13

How to Memorize the Biblical Narrative

One practical and immediate way to develop a deeper appreciation of Scripture and to thread it into the warp and woof of our imagination is to embed as much of the biblical narrative into our minds as possible. By having a detailed overview of the entire story of the Bible available for recall, we can better see what Graeme Goldsworthy calls the binding theme of the whole Bible—the kingdom of God, which he defines as "God's people in God's place under God's rule."[1]

Narrative is the most common form of writing in the Bible, comprising about 40 percent of the Old Testament and about half of the New Testament. The narrative-based books contain the main story line of the kingdom of God and include Genesis, Exodus, Numbers, Joshua, Judges, 1 and 2 Samuel, 1 and 2 Kings, 1 and 2 Chronicles, Ruth, Ezra, Nehemiah, Daniel, Jonah, Haggai, some of the prophetic writings, the Gospels (Matthew, Mark, Luke, John), and Acts.

Creating a Mental Overview

Turn to chapter 41, "How to Memorize Almost Anything," and familiarize yourself with the concepts of a memory palace (also called the "method of *loci*"), pegs, and nooks. Then return to this chapter to see how you can use it to create a detailed mental overview of the narrative books of the Bible. You'll soon be on your way to knowing hundreds of biblical people and events and where they fit into the story of the Bible—and passing this skill on to your children.

I've listed 30 events from the 50 chapters of Genesis. We'll apply the memorization technique to a handful of them to get you started.

1. God creates night and day.

2. God separates the water into atmospheric water and oceanic water.

3. God separates land from the oceanic waters and brings forth vegetation.

4. God reveals the sun, moon, and stars.

5. God creates birds and oceanic creatures.

6. God creates land animals.

7. God creates Adam and Eve.

8. God rests.

9. Adam and Eve eat from the tree of the knowledge of good and evil and leave the garden.

10. Cain kills Abel.

11. Noah builds an ark.

12. God makes a covenant with Noah.

13. Mankind builds the Tower of Babel.

14. God calls Abram to go to Canaan and Egypt.

15. Abram has a son, Ishmael. God changes Abram's name to Abraham.

16. God destroys Sodom and Gomorrah.

17. Lot's wife is turned into a pillar of salt.

18. Abraham's wife, Sarah, gives birth to Isaac.

19. God calls Abraham to sacrifice Isaac but provides a ram as substitute.

20. Sarah dies.

21. Isaac marries Rebekah.

22. Rebekah gives birth to Esau and Jacob.

23. Esau sells his birthright for a bowl of stew.

24. Jacob wrestles with God, and his name is changed to Israel.

25. Jacob's favorite son, Joseph, angers his brothers and is sold into slavery.

26. Potiphar's wife has Joseph thrown in jail.

27. Joseph interprets dreams for Pharaoh's cupbearer and baker and then Pharaoh.

28. Joseph is made prime minister of Egypt.

29. Joseph's brothers come to Egypt to buy grain.

30. Jacob dies and then Joseph dies.

Having read the book of Genesis (hopefully several times), you are familiar with the story. Yet the task of memorizing these events still seems daunting, doesn't it? Why start by memorizing the sequence of events of the fourth-longest book of the Bible? Wouldn't it be easier to start with a single verse from Scripture?

Surprisingly, no, it wouldn't. Most people will find they are able to memorize these 30 events easier and faster than they would a 30-word verse. You'll soon see why for yourself. In an hour, after you've read the following section and made a concerted effort to create the mental images, go back and read over the list, and you'll see you can remember almost all of them. With only a little more practice you'll soon be able to remember them with near perfect recall.

Let's get started on the first step in memorizing the story of the Bible, which begins in the Garden of Eden in Genesis 1 and ends in the New Jerusalem in Revelation 21.

Memorizing the Narrative of Genesis

The book of Genesis begins with creation (Genesis 1:1) and ends with the patriarch Joseph in a tomb in Egypt (Genesis 50:26). To help us remember the sequence of events that occur in between, we'll create image pegs that can be placed in the nooks and locations of your memory palace. Since the same memory palace can be used again and again for remembering different material (you'll use the same locations for each of the narrative books of the Bible you memorize), it helps to have a trigger that reminds you of a sequence. A useful one for this narrative is the first verse of the Bible: "In the beginning, God created the heavens and the earth." This will serve as the cue to recall the list of 30 items for this part of the biblical narrative.

Images and God's Actions

One of the challenges of making our unique and creative mental impressions is that significant parts of the biblical narrative involve direct action by God. The Bible warns us, however, against making images of our Creator (Exodus 20:4-6). As R.C. Sproul explains, "God is spiritual and invisible; nothing, therefore, in the earth or in the heavens above corresponds with His nature. Nothing can adequately or comprehensively represent Him."[2] We must therefore be careful to distinguish between images that represent actions *by* God and images *of* God.

For instance, in creating images to represent the actions of God in Genesis, I'll recommend the use of a pair of hands doing the creating. These images—which I'll repeatedly refer to as the representative hands—should be considered a representative abstraction used for creating a memorable mental image and should not be taken to represent "the hands of God." The distinction is subtle but necessary to avoid confusion about the intention of the imagery we are using for our model.

Location 1, Nook 1

Night and Day

In the first nook of our first location, we want to represent the action of Genesis 1:4: God "separated the light from the darkness." Picture our representative hand—a pair of massive hands at least three feet long—pulling a huge, bright lightbulb out of a large and extremely dark hole in the floor. It may help to imagine the words "day" and "night" written on the images.

Location 1, Nook 2

Atmospheric Water and Oceanic Water

In the second nook, we want the same representative hands to be placed on the top (palm facing down) and the bottom (palm facing up) of an extraordinarily large drop of water floating in midair. When the hands pull the drop apart, the top half turns into fluffy clouds that bounce on the ceiling while the bottom half splashes onto the floor, creating a waist-deep expanse of ocean. Try to hear the ocean water splashing about and the clouds dripping rain into the water below.

Location 1, Nook 3

Land and Vegetation

In the third nook, the representative hands will reach into the ocean water (which has seeped over from nook 2) and wipe it away until a large section of land appears in the middle. Have one hand reach down into the dirt and quickly pull up a large fruit tree (Genesis 1:12), an action that causes some of the fruit to fall and bounce on the ground. As a hand pulls the tree to the ceiling, picture grass growing in the rest of the dirt and the ocean water lapping around the edges of the dry ground.

Location 2, Nook 1

The Sun, Moon, and Stars

Now let's move on to your second location. For the first nook in this location, picture the representative hands reaching up to attach a comical-looking sun and moon to hooks or beams (sunbeams and moonbeams?) on a black expanse of the ceiling. Picture the sun giggling as the moon tries to shield its eyes from the glare. Once the sun and moon are firmly attached, one finger of the hand pokes holes in the dark ceiling, revealing the stars.

Location 2, Nook 2

Birds and Oceanic Creatures

In our next nook we are once again waist-deep in ocean water with clouds above us. One of the representative hands reaches up into the clouds and pulls out a peacock (or other colorful bird you find easy to remember) while the other reaches into the water and pulls out a great white shark. Picture the shark trying to take a bite of the peacock as the bird squawks and furiously flaps its plumage to avoid being eaten.

Location 2, Nook 3

Land Animals

Next we move to the last nook in the location. Imagine the representative hand reaching into a relatively small burlap sack and pulling out three or four large land animals, like cows and elephants. The hand struggles to pull the various animals out of the sack, and each animal lands on the floor with a *plop* and an annoyed grunt.

Location 3, Nook 1
Adam and Eve

We move on to our third location for the creation of our first parents. You likely have mental images of Adam and Eve already, so picture the hand reaching into a pile of dirt on the floor and pulling out a man. While one hand dusts him off, the other reaches into Adam's rib cage and pulls out a woman.

Location 3, Nook 2
God Rests

On the seventh day, God rested. To represent this action, we'll have the representative hands (which, keep in mind, are not God's hands but abstract representations of his actions) lie clasped on a pillow. The hands are emitting a deep snore.

Location 3, Nook 3
The Fall

We don't know what the fruit looked like, so feel free to picture whatever image pops into your head when you hear the word "fruit." For this example, we'll use an apple. Picture Adam and Eve in a garden about waist high (it can be sitting on a table or other object in your location). As they share an apple, they fall off the side of the garden and onto the floor (representing mankind's fall from grace).

Location 4, Nook 1
Cain Kills Abel

Even though we are familiar with the story of the first fratricide, we can forget who murdered whom. To help us remember, we'll use terms that sound similar as a helpful mnemonic device. Picture a man using a massive candy *cane* (Cain) to bludgeon another man who is lying on the ground and not *able* (Abel) to get up.

Location 4, Nook 2

Noah Builds an Ark

The story of Noah is one of the most common in all Western culture, so you probably already have a strong visual you can place in this nook. If nothing else comes to mind, imagine an old man loading animals into an ark as the rain begins to fall.

Location 4, Nook 3

God Makes a Covenant with Noah

The two cues we will use and tie together for this part of the story are the burnt offerings and the sign of the covenant (the rainbow). Imagine Noah setting fire to the feathers of a live peacock (perhaps the one from Location 2, Nook 2). As he does, a rainbow shoots from the plumage and creates an arch of color. (Bird-burning can be disturbing image, so it might help to make the visual less violent and more memorable by making it somewhat cartoonish.)

The author of *Rhetorica ad Herennium*, writing nearly a hundred years before Christ, says the duty of an instructor in mnemonics is to teach the method of making images, give a few examples, and then encourage the student to form his own.[3] When teaching "introductions," he says, one does not draft a thousand set introductions and give them to the student to learn by heart. Rather, one teaches him the method and then leaves him to his own inventiveness. That's the approach I'll take here.

Where to Go from Here

Creating your own images will certainly take time and effort. But here are a few suggestions to make the process less intimidating and time consuming.

Create Your Own Shorthand

Rather than writing everything out word for word, create shorthand that will remind you of the images you create and where you plan to place them in your memory palace. For example, you could write the details of "Location 3,

Nook 2: God Rests" like this: "Genesis :: 3/2 :: God Rests :: RH sleeping, snoring." Just remember the 3/2 refers to the location and nook, not the chapter and verse.

Divide the Workload

Image pegs you create yourself may be easier to remember, but for a complex task like this it may be helpful to share the workload. Instead of coming up with image pegs for every book of the Bible all by yourself, divide the tasks up among your family, friends, or small group. Work together to come up with a consensus for which events to include, but then have each person take one book and create a list of mental pegs for that part of the Bible. Be sure everyone shares the same code or shorthand to avoid confusion.

Set Aside Time Each Week for This Task

Use the techniques we covered in this series to schedule a time to accomplish this task. You gain no benefit from merely agreeing that memorizing the biblical narrative would be spiritually helpful—you must make time to accomplish this task and to help your child memorize the narrative. Isn't it worth 20 minutes of your time each week to embed the entire Bible story line into your imagination and your child's?

PART 2

SKILLS AND HABITS FOR INTERACTING WITH GOD

14

How to Pray

How would you answer if your child were to ask, "What is prayer?" Most parents might say prayer is talking to God, mostly to ask for what we need.

This is partially true, but a piece is missing. And if we don't include this missing element, we will fail to understand the purpose and role of prayer.

In Jeremiah, God tells the Israelites, "Call to me and I will answer you and tell you great and unsearchable things you do not know" (Jeremiah 33:3). This means that God's revelation is connected to our prayer.

Tim Keller further explains how prayer is connected to God's revelation:

> What is prayer, then, in the fullest sense? Prayer is continuing a conversation that God has started through his Word and his grace, which eventually becomes a full encounter with him...The power of our prayers, then, lies not primarily in our effort and striving, or in any technique, but rather in our knowledge of God.[1]

This is why, as Donald Whitney says, "of all the Spiritual Disciplines, prayer is second only to the intake of God's Word in importance."[2] Prayer is second in importance because it relies on our knowledge of God, which comes from reading or hearing his Word. Without engagement with the Bible, our prayers are lacking. It's like having a phone conversation in which the other person can hear us but we can't hear them. This means prayer starts not with what we say but with listening to God, by reading the Bible or hearing it read.

Now that we have the missing piece in place, we can offer a more robust definition:

> Prayer is an ongoing conversation with God in which we respond to his Word by worshiping and praising him, by confessing our sins, and by asking him to fulfill our needs and the desires of our heart.

That's the first thing we should know about prayer. The second thing we should know is that prayer is a learnable skill, and the best teacher we could ask for is Jesus.

The first people to recognize this fact were Jesus's own disciples. When they asked him to teach them to pray, he responded without hesitation, giving them a simple model for how his followers—including us—should pray.

> Father,
>
> your name be honored as holy.
>
> Your kingdom come.
>
> Give us each day our daily bread.
>
> And forgive us our sins,
>
> for we ourselves also forgive everyone
>
> in debt to us.
>
> And do not bring us into temptation (Luke 11:1-4 CSB).

When we examine this prayer, we discover an underlying template: the Five-Focus Framework.[3] The Lord's Prayer contains five areas of focus, each one asking for God's will to be done.

Focus 1: That God's name be honored—the focus on his everlasting glory ("Father, your name be honored as holy").

We honor God with our lips by praising him for all he has done, from creating the universe to giving us life to sending his Son to die on the cross for our sins. But we also must honor God as holy by living in obedience to his commands, which we learn by reading the Bible.

Focus 2: That God's kingdom come—the focus on his eternal will ("Your kingdom come").

As we've noted before, Graeme Goldsworthy describes the kingdom of God, the binding theme of the whole Bible, as "God's people in God's place under God's rule."[4] To pray that his "kingdom come" means we are asking that all believers—including us—be brought more fully under God's rule.

Focus 3: That God's provision is given—the focus on our present ("Give us each day our daily bread").

What do you need right now? Whether it's material needs, such as food and shelter, or emotional needs, such as peace or comfort, you can go to God and ask for them. This is known as a prayer of supplication. We should also ask God to intercede for others by giving them what they need. This is known as a prayer of intercession. We should teach our children to regularly include both supplication and intercession in their prayers.

Focus 4: That God's forgiveness is granted—the focus on our past ("Forgive us our sins, for we also forgive everyone who sins against us").

The first step in this focus is to consider whether you need to forgive anyone. Jesus says that if we do not forgive others their sins, our Father will not forgive ours (Matthew 6:15). Next, be both general and specific, asking God to forgive your sinful patterns of behavior as well as individual sins. Think about the past 24-hour period and identify and name particular sins you need to confess. Also, during this focus, make it a regular habit of asking the Holy Spirit to convict you of the sin in your life.

Focus 5: That God's deliverance will be provided—the focus on our future ("And do not bring us into temptation").

The Bible makes it clear God never tempts us (James 1:13). The desire to do evil by disobeying God is already within us because we are sinners. What this verse means is that we should ask God to protect us from giving in to such temptations, and we will continue to obey him in the future.

While each of your daily prayer sessions should include at least one of these focuses, be sure to pray about all five focuses over the course of each day.

Before you try to teach this framework to your child, make it a part of your life. Model it for your child by praying out loud in front of them and showing them what prayer should look like, just as Jesus did for his disciples.

How to Be Obedient to God

Few issues in modern Christian life are more misunderstood (or ignored) than the issue of biblical obedience. Some believers think obedience is optional, while others confuse it with legalism. Neither of these is true. Obedience is necessary for us to know and love God and for us to love our neighbors. Understanding obedience is thus essential not only for developing a biblical worldview but for living as a Christian.

What Obedience Is (and Is Not)

Obedience in the biblical sense is the grateful response to God's Word that leads us to submit to his authority and do his will. We have an obligation to obey God because he has authority over our lives. We know how to obey God because he has made his commandments known to us through Scripture. We can obey God because he has given us the power, through our union with Christ and the indwelling of the Holy Spirit, to do all he requires of us.

Obedience is not legalism—which is trying to win God's favor or impress others by doing certain things (or not doing them) without considering the condition of our hearts before God.[1] We don't earn God's favor by obeying him, nor can obedience gain us salvation. Only faith in the atoning work of Jesus on the cross can save us from God's wrath (Romans 5:9). We obey because we love God and desire to please him, not because we're trying to earn our way into heaven.[2]

Obedience Is Necessary to Love God, Know God, and Love Our Neighbor

Jesus states this point clearly when he says, "If you love me, keep my commands" (John 14:15). The apostle John also makes clear that only through obedience can we come to know God:

> We know that we have come to know him if we keep his commands. Whoever says, "I know him," but does not do what he commands is a liar, and the truth is not in that person. But if anyone obeys his word, love for God is truly made complete in them. This is how we know we are in him: Whoever claims to live in him must live as Jesus did (1 John 2:3-6).

Notice how blunt John is in claiming we are lying if we claim to know Christ and yet do not keep his commands. If we are not obedient, we do not truly know or love God.

John also makes clear that obedience is necessary to love others with the love of Christ:

> I am not writing you a new command but one we have had from the beginning. I ask that we love one another. And this is love: that we walk in obedience to his commands. As you have heard from the beginning, his command is that you walk in love (2 John 5-6).

How to Become More Obedient

If we want to become more obedient to God, four words can guide our way: fill, commit, read, and seek.

Fill. We obey not because we get something out of it (though we usually will gain peace, contentment, understanding, and more) but because we love God. Fill your heart with the love of the Lord. Spend some time each day reflecting on how you love Jesus, and that will motivate you to obey.

Commit. In 1729, William Law wrote *A Serious Call to a Devout and Holy Life*, in which he diagnosed a problem that plagues believers in every era:

> Now if you will stop here and ask yourself why you are not as pious as the primitive Christians were, your own heart will tell you that it is

neither through ignorance nor inability, but purely because you never thoroughly intended it.[3]

The primary reason we fail to obey God, as Law notes, is we rarely make a conscious intention to be obedient. Make a commitment every day to obey God in whatever he requires. Ask the Lord to give you the strength necessary to obey him in all things without hesitation.

Read. We cannot *obey* God's commands if we do not *know* what he commands. During your daily Bible reading, be on the lookout for God's commands. Make a list of commands that are applicable to all believers.

Seek. If in your daily Scripture reading you come across a specific command, be watchful for unique circumstances God may provide for you to obey. Have a plan for obedience, but be open, ready, and willing to obey in whatever ways God provides.[4]

Tips for Training Children

Obeying God by Obeying You

In his letter to the Ephesians, Paul addresses children: "Children, obey your parents because you belong to the Lord, for this is the right thing to do" (6:1 NLT). Paul is giving them a command from God—to be obedient to the Lord, they must obey their parents.

As parents we must be careful not to abuse this verse or use it merely to create compliant children. Many Bible translations use the phrase "obey your parents in the Lord," a qualification that means children should not—indeed, must not—obey an order if the father or mother is asking them to violate God's other commands. We also want to teach that their motivation must be out of a love for Jesus. They must obey what he commands, including his command to obey you, because they love him.

Let them also know Paul says this is "the first commandment with a promise: If you honor your father and mother, 'things will go well for you, and you will have a long life on the earth'" (Ephesians 6:2-3 NLT).

Obeying You So They Will Know How to Obey God

God requires children to obey their parents even before they are fully able to understand why. Once they become believers, they will fully understand that their motivation should be out of love for God and a desire to please him. But they are to obey you long before that time comes. Indeed, by obeying you, toddlers gain the experience that will teach them to obey God, as John Piper explains:

> Children need to obey before they can process obedience through faith. When faith comes, the obedience which they have learned from fear and reward and respect will become the natural expression of faith. Not to require obedience before faith is folly. It's not loving in the long run. It cuts deep furrows of disobedient habits that faith must then not infuse, but overcome.[5]

The Effects of Disobedience

All our sins affect other people because all sin transforms us into ungodly, unloving creatures. This is as true for toddlers as it is for adults. The consequences of our own sin affect those around us, so when we refuse to obey God's commands, we will affect their lives, either directly or indirectly.

Make it a practice to explain to your child that when they fail to obey God's commands, they are not only disappointing Jesus, they are hurting the other people they love and care about. Help them clearly see how their actions affect people in ways they may not have considered.

What God Commands

During your Bible reading, as you identify the commands of God, think through how they can be applied by your child. Make sure they understand that while some commands address their individual behavior, others empower them to be ambassadors of God's kingdom (see, for example, Matthew 9:37-38).

16

How to Overcome Sin

aul says that because we are made alive in Christ we are to put sin to death (Colossians 3:5). Putting sin to death is a daily task for all Christians. As the Puritan theologian John Owen said, "Be always at it while you live; cease not a day from this work; be killing sin or it will be killing you."

We must, as Paul says, put to death whatever belongs to our earthly nature. But if we use the phrase "killing sin," we could give the wrong impression. Not every indwelling sin can be killed during our lifetime. Sin is a like a horror movie monster that is killed repeatedly and yet returns time and time again.

Rather than using the phrase "killing sin," it's more useful to talk of "overcoming sin." To overcome is to get the better of something or someone in a struggle or conflict—to conquer or defeat.

Few Christians have thought more deeply or written more fruitfully about the process of overcoming sin than Owen, so we'll use his explanation of what overcoming sin is and is not.[1]

First, what overcoming sin is *not*.

Overcoming Sin Is Not Perfection

Jesus commands, "Be perfect...as your heavenly Father is perfect" (Matthew 5:48). Does this mean we can become perfect in the sense of being free from all sin? R.C. Sproul offers this explanation:

> Theoretically, the answer to that is yes. The New Testament tells us that with every temptation we meet, God gives us a way to escape that temptation. He always gives us enough grace to overcome sin. So sin

in the Christian life, I would say, is inevitable because of our weakness and because of the multitude of opportunities we have to sin. But on a given occasion, it is never, ever necessary. So in that sense, we could theoretically be perfect, though none of us is.[2]

While the goal of our life should be to overcome all sin—to be morally perfect—we should not let that overwhelm us. We can be grateful for the victory over sin in our life and the lives of our children even though we will not reach the state of moral perfection during our time on earth.

Overcoming Sin Is Not Concealing Sin

We can fool others (and sometimes even ourselves) into thinking we're no longer enslaved to specific sins. But no matter how hard we try to conceal our sin, God knows the truth.

Overcoming Sin Is Not Creating a Quiet Nature

Christianity is not Zen Buddhism. Overcoming sin will not transform us into enlightened monks who are disconnected from the cares of this world. Overcoming sin will naturally affect our personality, but the process is not intended to change our natural temperament.

Overcoming Sin Is Not Diverting Sin

Sometimes we think we have overcome a sin by keeping ourselves distracted. For example, if you move to an uninhabited desert island, you are less likely to commit certain sins against other people. But if you leave the island and start sinning against your neighbor, you never overcame the sin in the first place. Diverting our attention or temporary inclination toward a sin is not the same as overcoming it.

Overcoming Sin Is Not Occasional Victory

After engaging in sin, we may repent and return to God, having won a temporary battle against our sin. This is laudable, but it is not the same as the ongoing process of overcoming sin.

Now let's look at what it means to overcome sin.

A Habitual Weakening of Sin

Overcoming sin involves constantly fighting against it. Paul says, "Those who belong to Christ Jesus have crucified the flesh with its passions and desires" (Galatians 5:24). Paul's use of the gruesome metaphor of crucifixion is intentional. When we "crucify the flesh," we are, as Owen notes, "taking away its blood and spirits that give it strength and power—the wasting of the body of death 'day by day.'"

Frequent Success

That we will not conquer all sin in our life does not mean we cannot expect to conquer specific sins. We may, with constant effort, be able to overcome sinful anger or lust or other sins that previously vexed us. In fact, if we are serious about the process of overcoming sin, we should expect to win many frequent and decisive battles.

How We Can Overcome Sin

Based on this understanding, we can define overcoming sin as the habitual, successful weakening of sin that involves constant warfare and contention against the flesh.[3]

How then do we go about this process? Again, we can look to Owen as our guide. The Puritan thinker created a list of nine steps we can take to prepare us to overcome sin in our life. Tim Challies summarizes them in his article "9 Steps to Putting That Sin to Death."[4]

1. *Evaluate whether a sin is especially deep-rooted and persistent.*

Think about which sins in your life are most dominant or most destructive. Make a list of the ones that have become deeply ingrained.

2. *Fill your mind and conscience with the guilt, the weight, and the evil of your sin.*

We are often tempted to let ourselves off the hook and downplay the seriousness of our sin. We should trust God will forgive us, but we also need to recognize the grave violation we have committed against the Lord.

3. *Load your conscience with the guilt of your sin.*

"Look to the gospel, not for forgiveness yet, but for the ultimate picture of the cost of your sin," says Challies. "See Christ suffering for your sin and don't turn away your gaze. Feel all of that. Feel the weight, the guilt of it."

4. *Long for deliverance from the sin.*

"Now you will rightly see the cost and guilt of your sin, and you will long to be delivered from it so God can be glorified in you. Long for it. Pant for it. Cry out for it," says Challies.

5. *Consider how this sin is amplified by your nature or temperament.*

> You need to consider whether there is something in your makeup that makes you especially prone to this sin. Some people come from whole families of alcoholics and it may be that there is some kind of predisposition to addiction within them. Or perhaps you were sinned against earlier in life and the sins that were committed against you seem to make you especially prone to a sin of your own. Though these things may be true, you cannot allow them to excuse your sin. Instead, allow them to further convince you of your weakness and your desperate need for God's strength. Being predisposed toward a certain sin puts the burden on you to fight even harder against it, to destroy it even more completely, and to be especially vigilant in watching out for its reappearance.

6. *Contemplate the occasions in which this sin breaks out and guard against them.*

Think about the times when you are most prone to give in to temptations. Are you most likely to engage in gossip around certain friends? Do you give in to lust late at night while watching television or movies? Be honest with yourself about your weakness and put guardrails in place to help you avoid such situations.

7. *Battle hard against the first awakenings of that sin.*

If we regularly engage in a sin, we can almost always identify the point at which we know what we are doing is wrong, and yet we consciously choose to give in to the temptation. By applying more effort at this weak point, by crying out to God for help when we reach this stage, we can increase our ability to flee such temptations.

8. *Meditate on God to see his glory and your desperate inability.*

Filling our minds with the glory of God and reflecting on our own union with Christ help us to recognize we cannot overcome sin by our efforts alone. We are weak, but he is strong. We are incapable, but he is able. Meditating on this reality can help us see how much we must rely on God to transform us and protect us from our weakness.

9. *Expect to hear God speak peace to your soul (but do not speak it to yourself until he does).*

"Let God speak it through his Word or through his people," says Challies. "When he does, listen. But do not speak it to yourself too soon or you will be deluding yourself, and will go straight back into your sin."

Tips for Training Children

Understanding the Concept of Sin

For younger children, a helpful and simple definition of sin is, "Doing things our way instead of God's way." Walk them through various Bible stories—starting with Adam and Eve in the Garden of Eden—to show that doing things our way instead of God's way hurts and angers God, separates us from him, and leads to negative consequences, including death. Explain that Jesus died to take away the worst effects (our eternal separation from God), and if we love Jesus, we will avoid doing things our way and instead strive to do things God's way.

Temptation and Sin

As used in the Bible, the term "temptation" simply means to test or prove and has no negative connotation.[5] As Owen explained, temptation is "anything that, for any reason, exerts a force or influence to seduce and draw the mind and heart of man from the obedience which God requires of him to any kind of sin."[6] In child-friendly language, we can say temptation is anything that leads us to do things our way instead of God's way.

Being tempted is not sinful, as Jesus was himself tempted (Mark 1:12-13) but did not sin (Hebrews 4:15). God can allow us to undergo trials in which we are tempted to sin (Luke 11:4). But while the trial may be from God, the temptation to sin is not. God would never tempt someone to disobey him (James 1:13-14).[7]

"Resist, Flee, Pray"

The optimal strategy for overcoming sin is to avoid giving in to temptation in the first place. And God will always provide a way to escape temptation—we just need to resist, flee, and pray.

Resist. The apostle James says, "Resist the devil, and he will flee from you" (James 4:7). This usage is a military metaphor—James is urging us to stand our ground against Satan's attacks. Teach your child that they "resist the devil" when they refuse to surrender to the impulse to do things they know are wrong or that make God sad.

Flee. Sometimes the best way to stand our ground is to run away. In several places the Bible tells us the best way to resist temptation is to flee from it. Paul says to flee from sexual immorality (1 Corinthians 6:18), idolatry (1 Corinthians 10:14), the love of money (1 Timothy 6:10), and the evil desires of youth, or youthful immaturity (2 Timothy 2:22).

Teach your child that the best means of fleeing temptation is often to physically remove themselves (run away) from a situation that leads them to do things their own (wrong) way or from people who encourage them to behave in a way God says we should not.

Pray. Scripture makes it clear that God will not let us be tempted beyond what we can bear, and when we are tempted, he will provide a way out so we can endure it (1 Corinthians 10:13). Teach your child that if they will cry out to God in times of temptation, he will give them a way to resist, flee, or overcome the temptation to do things their way rather than God's way.

17

How to Develop Trust in God

What do parents most want for their children? Most parents across the globe would probably say they want their children to be happy. Happiness is certainly an admirable objective, but Christian parents should want something even more. We should want our children to trust God.

That may seem like an unusual priority. After all, shouldn't we want our children to *love* God? Absolutely. We should want them to love God with all their heart and with all their soul and with all their mind (Matthew 22:37). And the best way we can be sure they love God—truly love the Lord with all their being—is for them to trust him.

Trusting God is the attitude of our heart, soul, and mind in which we have complete faith in the goodness, power, and sufficiency of God. It's also a skill that must be learned and a habit to be developed.

We must develop our trust in the Lord because we don't fully trust him to know what we need most or to give it to us. If we did, we'd never be tempted to sin. If we truly believed God was always leading us in the right direction, we'd never balk at following him in complete obedience.

But we don't fully trust him. We become anxious because we fear he won't take care of us. We become doubtful because we can't see how he is in control. We become rebellious because we think we know what we need more than he does. We don't fully trust him because we're sinners.

Your child is a sinner too, of course. But by instilling the habit of trusting God, you can set them on a path that will lead not only to their sanctification but to their true happiness. For trusting in the Lord increases hope, and the hope of the righteous brings joy (Proverbs 10:28 ESV).

How do we develop the habit of trusting God? In four primary ways: reading Scripture, remembrance, patience, and obedience.

Reading Scripture

On almost every page of the Bible we can hear God whispering to us, "Trust me." The entire narrative of Scripture is telling us about God—who he is, what he has done, and what he will do. God's promises to us are prime examples of him teaching us to trust him. By some counts, the Bible includes about 8,000 such promises.[1] We find the first promise in Genesis 3:15 (and its fulfillment in Galatians 4:4; Luke 2:7; and Revelation 12:5) and the last promise in the two concluding verses of the Bible: "He who testifies to these things says, 'Yes, I am coming soon.' Amen. Come, Lord Jesus" (Revelation 22:20-21).

Some of the promises are intended for us, though most were specific promises made to individuals or to groups of believers in ancient times. But all the promises teach us something about the trustworthiness of God, as Barnabas Piper points out:

> A promise tells a little bit about who God is and what He will do. It is anchored in His holiness, goodness, power, and sovereignty. It is based on his omnipotence and omniscience. And it will come to pass in a way only God knows and ordains.[2]

By frequently reading the Bible and seeing how God fulfills his promises, we keep God's character and attributes in our heart and mind.

Remembrance

In reading the Bible we are reminded of how God has kept faith with his people. We can also build trust by reminding ourselves how he has been faithful to us. Our trust in God weakens when we forget how often he has answered our prayers, protected us from harm, or allowed us to avoid the full consequences of our own sinful actions. Looking back to see how he has been faithful in our lives can strengthen our faith as we look forward to the future.

Patience

Trust almost always includes an element of waiting. For example, if you trust your spouse will be picking up the children from school later in the day, you are trusting something will happen in the future. You assume, based on your spouse's character and their reliability in the past, that at the right time (after school) they will fulfill this future obligation (picking up the kids). Your trust may be so implicit you don't give it a second thought.

Trust in God often contains a similar element of waiting. For example, the prophet Isaiah said, "I will wait for the LORD, who is hiding his face from the descendants of Jacob. I will put my trust in him" (Isaiah 8:17). Isaiah had no idea how long he'd have to wait, but it didn't matter—he had implicit trust in God.

Sometimes we wait on the Lord because the timing between what we seek and what he will provide is not yet aligned. But oftentimes the waiting is for our direct benefit, to teach us patience so our trust in him will grow. "Biblically, waiting is not just something we have to do until we get what we want," says John Ortberg. "Waiting is part of the process of becoming what God wants us to be."[3]

Obedience

Trusting God leads to obedience, and obedience leads to greater trust in God. This occurs in a three-step process. The first step is the *belief* stage, in which we believe a command or principle in the Bible is true. Our belief leads us to the *action* stage, the step in which we act on the belief by obeying Christ. Because the Bible is always truthful, our obedience confirms the truth of the belief, leading to the final stage—*increased belief and trust.*

A prime example of someone following this pattern of belief to action to knowledge to greater belief is the royal official in Cana who had heard about the healing power of Jesus (John 4:46-47). The official came to Jesus to heal his son, who was dying. But rather than go to the child, Jesus gives the official a command to be obeyed: "Go," Jesus replied, "your son will live" (verse 50).

Imagine being in that situation. Would you have trusted your child was healed, or would you have wanted Jesus to come in person to make sure it happened? The official didn't hesitate—he simply obeyed. And before he even got home he received confirmation his son had been healed.

The man's trust in Jesus was rewarded with knowledge of Jesus's power and trustworthiness. Notice the reaction to the news: "He and his whole household believed" (verse 53). The official already believed, of course, but now he had confirmation his belief was true—which caused him to believe and trust God even more.

Tips for Training Children

Teach Them What the Bible Says About Trusting God

While it's good for them to hear from you that they should trust God, hearing it from God himself is even better. Have them read and perhaps memorize such verses as Psalm 5:11; 37:5; 46:1; 118:8; and Proverbs 3:5-6; 30:5.

Teach Them Family Stories About Trusting God

The stories children hear about their family will last with them a lifetime. Be sure you are including stories about how God brought individual members of the family through hard times or how putting your trust in God has affected the family.

Teach Them How to Wait on the Lord

Because they have lived for so brief a time on the earth, children tend to have a skewed perception of time. As older, mature Christians, we can understand why God could take years to respond to our pleading. But for children, especially small children, a few years can seem—quite literally— like a lifetime. Help them understand waiting on the Lord is not about watching the clock or calendar, but rather about changing our attitude and expectations.

Teach Them to Obey God

Children need to know that when it comes to our interactions with God, obedience must take precedence and will sometimes precede trust. If we're waiting to obey God until after he answers our prayers, then we are making the Creator of the universe subject to our will. Small children need to know we serve a big God who never fails us and knows more than we know. We can trust him because he loves and cares about us even more than we can love and care about ourselves.

PART 3

SKILLS AND HABITS FOR INTERACTING WITH OTHER PEOPLE

18

How to Handle Criticism

Proverbs says, "In the end, people appreciate honest criticism far more than flattery" (Proverbs 28:23 NLT). Honest criticism can provide opportunities for our growth, helping us become stronger, more confident people. To help a child learn how to handle criticism and use it to their advantage, encourage them to ask four questions: What is the criticism? How does it apply? Does it matter? How should I respond?

Tips for Training Children

What Is the Criticism?

We don't always say what we mean, and even when we do, we may not *understand* what we mean. We adults constantly struggle with this problem, and it's even more of an issue for children. For example, if someone tells a child, "You are slow," they may not understand whether they're being told they are moving slowly or they are mentally "slow." Or is the statement a misguided attempt at humor?

Rather than simply accepting the criticism—and incessantly pondering what it means—kids can learn to simply say, "I want to make sure I understand you. Is this what you're saying…?" Asking what the criticism is and seeking clarification gets the child into the habit of detaching from the criticism. A child trained to stop and ask, "What exactly did they mean?" will be better able to consider the criticism. They will also be less likely to respond emotionally.

Does It Apply?

Some criticism is obviously inaccurate and can be immediately dismissed. But criticism is often relative, and determining how it might apply to us depends on the context. In our example, the child may determine that since someone said, "You are slow" during a game of tag, the speaker was referring to physical speed.

To determine whether the criticism is accurate also depends on the context. Slow compared to whom? Slow compared to the other children playing the game? Tell the child that when they receive criticism, they can discuss it with someone they trust to help them determine if it is accurate and applicable.

Does It Matter?

This is the pivotal question when dealing with any criticism. A critique may be accurate and yet not matter. A child who is more interested in intellectual or artistic pursuits may not value athletic prowess, and so being told they are slow while playing tag may not be a concern.

Unfortunately, it's not always that simple. Children take most (if not all) criticism personally. Helping the child determine what matters to them can empower them to shrug off unimportant criticisms and to better deal with those that do matter.

How Should I Respond?

When teaching your child how to respond to criticism, carefully consider their attitude and emotions. You want to train the child to have a positive attitude, but don't be dismissive of their feelings. Even when it's wrapped in praise, direct criticism can be painful. Let the child know that the pang of sadness or depression is normal and acceptable, but that it shouldn't determine how they respond. Instead, they should have a template for responding to negative feedback. Here are some examples you can modify for your own child:

- Instead of getting angry, take a breath and respond, "I want to be sure I understand. Can you explain more what you meant?"

- Instead of crying, detach and respond, "Do you mind if I give this some thought and we can talk about it later?"

- Instead of denying it, pause and respond, "This comes as a surprise to me. Could you give me examples of what you mean?"

- Instead of blaming other people, focus on yourself and respond, "Can you tell me more about how you see the problem?"[1]

Next, help your child formulate their own plan for addressing the criticism. Is the issue something they can change? If so, what can they do differently? Is the issue something they cannot change? If so, how can they learn to accept the reality of the situation?

They should also take time to consider how they will respond to the person who criticized them and how that response might affect their relationship. Generally, their two best options are to express forgiveness or gratitude.

If the criticism is untrue or unhelpful, we must forgive our accusers just as Jesus forgives us. If the person is always critical of us, though, it may be a sign of an underlying problem. Let the child know that constant negativity isn't what God intends for our relationships and that if a friend or relative offers nothing but criticism, the child should ask an adult to intervene.

If the criticism was true and helpful, we should thank the person who confronted us. As Proverbs says, "Wounds from a friend can be trusted" (27:6). If it helps us grow as a person, we should thank God for putting in our lives the person who offered painful but necessary criticism.

19

How to Stand Up for Yourself

Assertiveness is the skill that allows us to stand up for our rights or the rights of others. It helps us to be treated fairly and to respectfully express our thoughts, feelings, needs, or desires. God-honoring assertiveness is the middle way between acting overly timid, which causes people to overlook our concerns, or overly aggressive, which leads us to appear abrasive or self-righteous.

The most important way to develop a child's assertiveness is to help them know they are image bearers of God, which gives them intrinsic worth and the right to be treated with respect.

Tips for Training Children

Filling in the Blanks

Assertiveness is a communication skill. Assertiveness includes some nonverbal elements, but it primarily requires that we express ourselves verbally. If a child is timid or aggressive, they may be unable to clearly formulate what they want to say in a way that can be conveyed clearly and respectfully.

As parents, we're tempted to save time and stress by filling in the blanks. We know from experience what our child is trying to say, so we don't require them to fully express themselves. By using this shortcut, though, we're not allowing the child to learn how to communicate their inner thoughts and needs. Let them express themselves as clearly as possible so they'll develop the confidence necessary to be assertive.

Verbal Scripts

You can help a child assert themselves in a healthy way by giving them broadly applicable verbal scripts. For example, to express a preference they could say, "If possible, I'd prefer…" This formula helps them clarify their preference while also acknowledging it may not be possible for their preference to be fulfilled.

To express their feelings, they could say, "When you…, I feel…" For instance, a child could use this to convey to an older sibling, "When you don't let me play with you, I feel lonely and left out."

By developing and using scripts like these, the child is relieved of some of the pressure of trying to determine what they want to say.

No one has a right to do wrong. We therefore should never assertively do anything that would dishonor our Creator. However, if we are asserting our right to express an opinion or ask to be treated in a way that is God-honoring, we should do so with humble boldness.

Role-Play Real-Life Scenarios

Sometimes a child needs to confront someone but is nervous about the reaction they might get. You can alleviate some of the concern by preparing them through role-playing. Have them say what they are thinking or feeling while you play the role of the person they are confronting.

Walk through several scenarios, starting with the best possible outcome and gradually working to the worst possible (realistic) reaction. If the child is unprepared for an adverse or even hateful response, they are less likely to be assertive in the future. Explain to the child that while they should stand up for themselves, they can't control other people's reactions.

No Borrowed Assertiveness

Imagine the following scenario. You're at a fellowship dinner at your church, and your child asks for a piece of cake. You are trying to teach your child to be more assertive with adults, so you walk them to the dessert table and say, "Ask Mrs. Johnson if you can have some cake." The child dutifully parrots the request, and in return Mrs. Johnson smiles and hands over a slice of chocolate cake.

What has the child learned? They've learned they can borrow your assertiveness. If you're standing beside them telling them what to say, you are being assertive, not the child. They intuitively understand this, which is why they'll often ask you to accompany them for such requests.

Encouraging the child to be assertive without your direct presence can be challenging for you and for them. But it's the only way they will develop their skill so people will respond to them and not the authority of their parent.

Patience as They Learn

Learning to be assertive takes practice, and if your child is naturally timid, it may require years of practice. Don't be discouraged or frustrated. Work on the skill at a pace fitting for the child. The goal is not to develop an assertive child but a child who will become an assertive adult.

20

How to Say You're Sorry

Saying "I'm sorry" shouldn't be difficult. But as pop music reminds us, it is often "Hard to Say I'm Sorry" and "Sorry Seems to Be the Hardest Word." The difficulty is apparent in the rise of the non-apology apology—sometimes called a nonpology or fauxpology—an apology in which we are not sorry for our actions but for the fact someone was offended ("I'm sorry you feel that way").

Before we can teach our children how to say they are sorry, we may need to review the hows and whys of apologizing.

Why We Need Apologies

The purpose of an apology is to seek reconciliation and restoration with someone we've hurt or wronged. By sincerely asking for forgiveness, we take an essential step in mending a rupture, however small, in a relationship. Even if we know the other person will forgive us, it is important we ask them directly.

Joseph's brothers provided us a prime example when they asked him to forgive them for selling him into slavery (Genesis 50:17). Joseph knew God had used their evil to bring about good, but their acknowledgment helped restore the broken relationship in their family.

Training your child to deliver an adequate, relationship-restoring apology is challenging. Unfortunately, that is only half the process. The other half is to help your child understand why the apology is necessary. Too often we parents believe by merely commanding an apology ("Tell your brother you're sorry!"), we have fulfilled our obligation to restore order. But such forced apologies tend to make the child resentful and leave the person who was wronged feeling bitter over the insincerity. The result may even be worse than before the forced apology by causing an even greater rift in the relationship.

Teaching the child why they need to apologize is more time consuming than simply telling them what to say, but it is absolutely necessary. Here again, a formula will be helpful—especially since this is likely to be a daily process for most parents.

Tips for Training Children

The Elements of the Apology

Beth Polin, coauthor of *The Art of the Apology*, defines an apology as a statement that includes one or more of six elements:[1]

- An expression of regret—this is usually the actual "I'm sorry"
- An explanation (not a justification)
- An acknowledgment of responsibility
- A declaration of repentance
- An offer of repair
- A request for forgiveness

A Helpful Format

To help your child incorporate these components into an apology, put them into a specific framework. Former elementary school teacher JoEllen Poon recommends a four-point formula.[2]

1. *I'm sorry for...* This part should be specific. Instead of making a generic statement ("I'm sorry I hurt your feelings"), the child should make it clear they understand why the apology is needed ("I'm sorry for saying I didn't want to be your friend").

2. *This is wrong because...* This part of the apology is more complex because it includes three of the elements from Polin's framework: an explanation, an acknowledgment of responsibility, and a declaration of repentance. For example, "This is wrong because you are a nice person and I do want to be your friend. I never should have said I didn't."

3. *In the future, I will...* Poon recommends using positive language—having the child say what they will do rather than what they won't do. For example, "In the future I will be more loving in how I speak to you."

4. *Will you forgive me?* The apology ends with an invitation for the person who was harmed to provide their own input and acknowledge, however tentatively, the slight will not have a long-term effect on the relationship.

Transform Justification into an Explanation

Many times we don't apologize because we believe we were justified in acting as we did. Help the child understand their action from the perspective of the person who was offended or wronged and then help them explain why they were wrong.

Have Them Explain Why It Shouldn't Happen Again

The process of acknowledging, repenting, and repairing is easier when the child can see the harm their action would have if they continued to do it. For example, "Hitting your little sister hurt her, and it will cause her not to feel safe around you. A big brother is expected to protect his little sister, not hurt her."

Ask for a Solution

Once the child understands why they are wrong and can see the broad context of their actions, they are more likely to understand why they need to apologize. Ask them what they should do next to resolve the situation. If they still don't understand why they need to express regret, larger issues may need to be uncovered.

Show Appreciation for Their Apology

Tell the child you appreciate their doing the right thing. Yes, it can be annoying to give a child praise for merely restoring the status quo and to reward them for doing what they should do automatically. But remember, you are attempting to develop a lifelong habit, and that positive reinforcement is a powerful way to help your child learn to reflect on their actions and deliver sincere apologies.

21

How to Forgive

When Jesus taught us to pray, he said we should ask God, "Forgive us our debts, as we also have forgiven our debtors" (Matthew 6:12). We forgive others because God has forgiven us. And just as Jesus taught us to pray, we should learn to forgive the way God forgives.

What is the pattern for God's forgiveness? Based on criteria outlined in Scripture, Chris Brauns defines God's forgiveness as "a commitment by the one true God to pardon graciously those who repent and believe so that they are reconciled to him, although this commitment does not eliminate all consequences." Using God's pattern for our own, Brauns defines human forgiveness as "commitment by the offended to pardon graciously the repentant from moral liability and to be reconciled to that person, although not all consequences are necessarily eliminated."[1]

Let's consider what this means for how we establish a habit of forgiving.

Forgiveness Requires Repentance

The idea that forgiving other people requires they be repentant and seek our forgiveness is surprisingly controversial. It shouldn't be, because forgiveness should lead to restoration, as John Stott makes clear:

> If a brother who has sinned against us refuses to repent, we should not forgive him. Does this startle you? It is what Jesus taught…"Forgiveness" includes restoration to fellowship. If we can restore to full and intimate fellowship with ourselves a sinning and unrepentant brother, we reveal not the depth of our love but its shallowness.[2]

True repentance is necessary for true forgiveness, which is necessary for true restoration.

Forgiveness Is Gracious

The starting point of our willingness and ability to forgive is the forgiveness of our own sins by a gracious God. We should regularly reflect on the many ways we have sinned against our Creator and then think about the price he paid so we could be forgiven and restored. When we focus on our gratitude for what God has done in forgiving our sins, we can more easily and graciously forgive those who sin against us.

Forgiveness Is Not Optional

Reflecting on how God has graciously forgiven us will often motivate us to forgive others. But when the hurt and pain is too deep and forgiveness seems impossible, we may need to remind ourselves that forgiving others is not optional—it's a prerequisite for the forgiveness of our own sins. As Jesus says, "If you forgive other people when they sin against you, your heavenly Father will also forgive you. But if you do not forgive others their sins, your Father will not forgive your sins" (Matthew 6:14-15).[3]

Forgiveness Doesn't Require Imprudence

We can forgive without forgetting the situation that caused the debt or harm. For instance, if someone has physically abused you in the past, you can forgive them without putting yourself in a situation where they can continue to abuse you. Forgiveness should lead us to seek reconciliation. But we are not required to put ourselves in danger. As Rose Sweet says, "While God commands us to forgive others, he never told us to keep trusting those who violated our trust or even to like being around those who hurt us."[4]

Forgiveness Does Not Negate Consequences

The willingness to forgive does not mean the forgiven will suffer no consequences for their action. Indeed, if a person is only seeking forgiveness to avoid the consequences of their actions, they may not be truly repentant. "Consequences are important for the sake of justice," says Brauns. "A willingness to accept consequences for sinful behavior is actually good evidence the offender truly is repentant."[5]

Tips for Training Children

Ask Them for Forgiveness

The only human who never needs to ask for forgiveness is Jesus. The rest of us sin against others and must seek forgiveness and reconciliation. This is especially necessary in the family. Just because we have been put in a position of authority over our children does not mean we do not sin against them. When we do, we should ask their forgiveness and seek reconciliation. In doing so, we not only restore their trust in us but model for them how forgiveness works.

Teach Them to Ask for Forgiveness

As they're developing the habit of learning to forgive, children should be made aware of how often they need forgiveness and how to ask for it. (See chapter 20, "How to Say You're Sorry.")

The Four Promises of Forgiveness (Younger Children)

When we forgive someone, we should make four promises to ourselves:

- I promise I will think good thoughts about you and do good for you.
- I promise I will not bring up this situation and use it against you.
- I promise I will not talk to others about what you did.
- I promise I will be friends with you again.[6]

These promises can be summarized in a rhyme children can memorize:

Good thought

Hurt you not

Gossip never

Friends forever[7]

The Four Promises of Forgiveness (Older Children and Teens)

A similar formulation can be used for older children and teenagers. Ken Sande recommends we make four promises when we forgive someone:

- I will not dwell on this incident.
- I will not bring up this incident again and use it against you.
- I will not talk to others about this incident.
- I will not let this incident stand between us or hinder our personal relationship.[8]

Children can also use this as a checklist to search their heart and determine whether they have truly forgiven someone (for example, "Do I continue to dwell on the incident?" "Do I gossip with others about the incident?")

In applying these promises, children of every age should be taught to use discernment. If someone has abused them or caused them harm, they should talk about the incident with an adult—even if they have forgiven the person. Similarly, they may have troubling memories about an incident that was traumatic or that caused a severe rupture in a relationship. These promises are usually useful when we need to forgive, but there will be exceptions. Children should feel comfortable asking you to help them know how the promises apply to their situation.

PART 4

SKILLS AND HABITS
FOR DISCERNMENT AND
DECISION-MAKING

22

How to Develop Your Conscience

Imagine you could give your child a device that would let them know when they are about to violate their moral standards and prod them to do what is right. Fortunately, God has already given them just such a tool—their conscience.

We hear a lot about the conscience, but what exactly is it? The Greek term for the conscience occurs more than two dozen times in the New Testament and serves an important concept, particularly in the letters of Paul.

The conscience does not serve as a judge or a legislator; that is a modern take on the concept. Instead, in the biblical sense, conscience serves as a *witness* and can sometimes induce an inner dialogue to tell us what we already know (Romans 2:15; 9:1). But more often it merely makes its presence known through our emotions. When we conform to the values of our conscience, we feel a sense of pleasure or relief. But when we violate the values of our conscience, we feel anguish or guilt. John MacArthur describes conscience as "a built-in warning system that signals us when something we have done is wrong. The conscience is to our souls what pain sensors are to our bodies: it inflicts distress, in the form of guilt, whenever we violate what our hearts tell us is right."[1]

The First Rule of Conscience

The most important thing your child should know about their conscience is that it is *always* to be subordinate to and informed by the revealed Word of God. To develop their conscience, they must first know what God says about how we should live and act. Conscience is an important tool, but it cannot be our final ethical authority because it is changeable and fallible, unlike God's revealed Word. Too often we reverse the order and attempt to use our conscience to judge God and his Word. Many Christians claim, for example, "I could not worship a God who would say [a clear statement from the Bible]" or "I couldn't believe in a God who would do [something the Bible clearly says God did]." In making such statements, they may be appealing to their conscience, but their conscience is not being informed by God.

A person's conscience may cause them to question an *interpretation* of Scripture. But our conscience can never legitimately judge a holy God or his holy Word. When we find ourselves thinking, "Did God really say?" when the Bible clearly says he did, then we know the serpent is speaking, not the Savior (Genesis 3:1).

The Second Rule of Conscience

The second most important thing to know about conscience is that to willfully act against conscience is *always* a sin.

Our conscience should always be informed by what God has said. But what if we are mistaken about what the Bible commands or forbids? What if, for example, I believe the Bible forbids any form of dancing—and yet I go square dancing every Saturday night. Is that a sin? In that case it would be a sin to square dance since I would be behaving in a way *I thought God says is wrong*.

Imagine your child is at a friend's house and sees a wallet lying on the floor. Thinking it is their playmate's wallet, they reach in and take a $5 bill. Later they realize it wasn't their friend's wallet but their own, which had fallen out of their pocket. Would they be guilty of theft, even though it was their own money they took? Yes, since they had *intended to do wrong*. They had intended to steal even though they were mistaken about the object of the theft. As Paul says, "For whatever does not proceed from faith is sin" (Romans 14:23 ESV). R.C. Sproul offers this comment:

> If we do something that we think is sin, even if we are misinformed, we are guilty of sin. We are guilty of doing something we believe to be wrong. We act against our consciences. That is a very important principle. Luther was correct in saying, "It is neither right nor safe to act against conscience."

Tips for Training Children

Respect Their Conscience

Imagine a father who is an avid hunter and wants to introduce his daughter to his lifelong passion. She refuses because she believes it would be a sin for her to kill small animals. What should the father do? The answer is simple: He should respect her conscience. The daughter may be wrong about hunting being a sin, but it would be a sin for her to violate her conscience by killing animals.

As Sproul says, the "conscience can excuse when it ought to be accusing, and it also can accuse when it should be excusing." While we should challenge misperceptions of what the Bible commands and forbids, we should be careful about encouraging people who are not yet mature in the faith or are underdeveloped in knowledge of Scripture from acting in ways that will violate their unformed or immature conscience.

Incentivize Their Conscience

When helping your child develop their conscience, make it easier for them to follow their internal guidance system than to ignore it and conceal their wrongdoing. For example, while they shouldn't be rewarded for engaging in bad behavior, it may be appropriate to lessen their punishment if they confess. Remember, the long-term goal is to help them develop a habit so that listening to their conscience will become second nature. We may need to sacrifice short-term moral lessons to develop a robust conscience that will guide them for a lifetime.

23

How to Know God's Will for Your Life

How do we know God's will for our life? How will our child know whether God wants them to go to college and, if so, where should they should attend? How will they know whom to marry or what career to pursue?

Questions about knowing God's will are some of the most pressing in the Christian life. But we often misunderstand where to find the answer because we don't fully understand what the Bible says about God's will. Here are a few concepts you should know.

The Two Wills of God

Theologians identify two general wills God expresses in the Bible: decretive and preceptive.

God's Decretive Will

"Decretive" means having the force of a decree or an official order given by a person with power and authority, such as a king or sovereign.[1] God's decretive will is sometimes described as the sovereign will by which God has the power to bring to pass whatever he pleases by his divine decree. A prime example of this is that it was God's will that Joseph be kidnapped by his brothers, sold into slavery, and thrown into prison, and that he would rise to the second in command of all Egypt and save the people from famine (Genesis 37–50). We are under no obligation to try to discern God's decretive will because he will reveal it when he is ready—often after what he has decreed has come to pass.

God's Preceptive Will

"Preceptive" means expressing a commandment or direction given as a rule of action or conduct. God's preceptive will is also known as his revealed will since it relates to the revealed commandments of God's law written in Scripture and on our conscience. The Ten Commandments are the most famous examples of God's preceptive will. This is the most direct way we can know God's will for our life. We therefore have an obligation to search Scripture to discover what God requires of us so we may be obedient to his will.

What About a "Will of Direction"?

You might be thinking something is missing. "How do I know God's will about where I should live, what job I should take, and whom I should marry? Isn't there a secret 'will of direction'?" The answer is no, there's not, as Kevin DeYoung explains:

> Does God have a secret will of direction that He expects us to figure out before we do anything? And the answer is no. Yes, God has a specific plan for our lives. And yes, we can be assured that He works things for our good in Christ Jesus. And yes, looking back we will often be able to trace God's hand in bringing us to where we are. But while we are free to ask God for wisdom, He does not burden us with the task of divining His will of direction for our lives ahead of time. The second half of that last sentence is crucial. God does have a specific plan for our lives, but it is not one that He expects us to figure out before we make a decision.[2]

That answer may surprise you, but it's thoroughly biblical. Nothing in the Bible implies God has a secret set of instructions and if you don't ask for them your life will be a mess. The Bible does make clear that we are to seek his preceptive will—to know and follow what he commands, including the command to "get wisdom, get understanding" (Proverbs 4:5).

This is both incredibly freeing and absolutely frightening. Making decisions would be easier if God wrote the direction for our life on a slip of paper and let us take a peek at it if we found the right way to ask. But God designed a better way for us to know what he wants for us: Seek him, obey his commands, seek wisdom, and then…make choices. DeYoung adds this:

> So go marry someone, provided you're equally yoked and you actually

like being with each other. Go get a job, provided it's not wicked. Go live somewhere in something with somebody or nobody. But put aside the passivity and the quest for complete fulfillment and the perfectionism and the preoccupation with the future, and for God's sake start making some decisions in your life. Don't wait for the liver-shiver. If you are seeking first the kingdom of God and His righteousness, you will be in God's will, so just go out and do something.[3]

Tips for Training Children

Teach Them the "Essentials" Are Essential

The freedom God gives us to make decisions for our lives can be easily misunderstood, especially by children and teens. We are not free *from* constraints, but free *to* know and follow God's revealed will. And most of his will is the same for everyone, as Karl Vaters explains:

> God's will for all of us includes loving God, loving others, being worshippers, telling the truth and so on. So, 90 percent of what God wants us to do is the same for all of us.
>
> On the other side, God's will never includes an exemption from character traits like integrity, or an allowance for cruelty. So, 90 percent of what we're *not* supposed to do is the same for everyone, too.
>
> Between the do's and the don'ts, the overwhelming majority of God's will is the same for everyone.
>
> So why do so many believers get all stressed out about finding God's will for their life?
>
> I believe it's because most of us tend to overplay the importance of God's specific will for our life, while underestimating the value of knowing and doing God's universal will for all our lives.
>
> We often want to skip past the 90 percent (the Essentials) and jump straight to the 10 percent (the Specifics).[4]

By teaching our children to focus on "the Essentials" they'll be better prepared for the "Specifics" of their own life.

Eight Considerations for Discerning God's Will

We should teach our children that discerning God's will for our lives means seeking out what he has revealed in the Bible (his preceptive will) and using wisdom to make decisions. David Sills identifies eight components to keep in mind to "make the best decision for the next step in your life."[5] Here are the eight considerations and some questions you can consider on each:[6]

1. *Know God.* Am I more concerned about knowing God's will for my life than I am about knowing God?

2. *Know his Word.* Have I searched Scripture to find God's revealed will?

3. *Prayer.* Do I frequently ask God to guide me and to open my eyes to his revealed will?

4. *Counsel.* Who are the wise and godly men and women from whom I should be seeking counsel?

5. *Life experiences.* Why has God given me this unique set of life experiences? What could it reveal about what I should do with my life?

6. *Circumstances.* What do my circumstances reveal about what I should do next? Are there obvious needs or opportunities that could be pointing me in a certain direction?

7. *Timing.* Is the timing right for me to respond? Is it wise to wait where I am or more prudent for me to take a decisive step forward?

8. *Desire.* What do I want to do? If I delight in the Lord, what would be the desire of my heart (Psalm 37:4)? How do I most want to serve God?

When your child is considering significant decisions in their life, walk with them through these eight considerations and discuss how each affects their choice.

24

How to Make Better Decisions

The average adult reportedly makes 70 conscious decisions every day.[1] That means we make a decision, on average, four times every waking hour, or about once every 15 minutes. Of course, most of the decisions we make are trivial—what clothes we'll wear, what we'll eat for breakfast, and so on. But we frequently need to make substantive decisions that may have a profound effect on our lives or the lives of others. Because of the significance of decision-making, we need to develop the habit of doing it well—and teaching our children how they can make better decisions.

The decision-making process is circular: The decisions we make are determined by our worldview, but they also help shape our worldview. Our day-to-day decisions to hear God's Word and to obey his commands lead us to become wise and thus able to make better decisions. This leads us to the first of 12 steps in a process for making godly decisions.[2]

1. *Commit to seeking God's will.* Commit to seeking God's will by praying he will guide you through each step of the decision-making process. Search the Bible for relevant commands and principles, and obey all he asks you to do.

2. *Classify the question.* Is this a generic type of problem or something unique? While many of the decisions we need to make will be on questions unique to us, the problem itself is probably generic. That means someone else you know has probably had to make a similar decision and may be able to provide prudent advice or guidance.

3. *Define the problem.* Once we determine whether the problem is unique or generic, we then need to drill down and define it clearly. For example, you

might initially think the decision you are making is whether to take a new job when the real problem you are grappling with is whether a change that would advance your career is worth leaving your extended family, friends, and local church to move to a new city.

4. *Understand the specifications for the decision.* You need to be clear with yourself what specifications you need to meet to make a wise decision. While this may appear to be obvious, we may think we've decided an issue when the outcome does not meet our long-term specifications or goals. For instance, our long-term goal may be to marry a spouse who loves and honors God. But we may decide to accept a marriage proposal from an unbeliever, thinking we can convert them during the engagement period. In such a case we would fail to meet the specification for a decision, and we would be creating future problems.

5. *Determine whether the decision is covered by a command.* Has God provided a clear course of action in Scripture? Is there a clear command about what should be done? In the case of marrying someone who is not a Christian, the Bible is clear we should not be "unequally yoked" to an unbeliever (2 Corinthians 6:14). If the command is clear, our decision is also clear: We must obey God.

If the decision is not clearly covered by a command, we can consider whether we can determine a principle based on analogy or indirect extension of a related principle (see chapter 8, "How to Apply Scripture to Your Life"). Sometimes, though, the decision—such as whether we should take a new job—is not going to be revealed simply through reading the Bible. In these cases, we must move to the next step.

6. *Gather relevant information.* What additional information do you need to make the decision? Do any specific obligations, such as to your spouse or children, affect the decision? Do you need to consider any specific data, such as the pros and cons? What are your personal desires? Are you excited about a certain outcome or nervous about what would happen if you chose a particular path? Collect as much information as you think is necessary to make a timely decision.

7. *Seek wise counsel.* As Proverbs states, "For lack of guidance a nation falls, but victory is won through many advisers" (11:14). Get input on the decision from mature and wise advisers.

8. *Process the information through your values and worldview.* To consistently

make wise and godly decisions, we must be becoming wise and godly people. If you have taken the time to develop the other habits in this book, you'll be equipped to make better decisions. If you are striving to be obedient to God, trusting in him, and seeking his will, then you'll have developed the values and worldview that will help your long-term decision-making be rooted in wisdom and courage.

9. *Identify your choices.* After you've gathered and processed the relevant information, you may find you have a broader range of choices than you originally considered. Don't let this paralyze the process. Pray for guidance and then narrow down your options to the ones you find most appealing or that will best solve the problem.

10. *Make a decision (or not).* Every prior step to this point is intended to give you clarity about your choice. But ultimately, you must make a decision—even if the decision is not to decide just yet. Recognize that the choice not to decide is itself a decision about how to address the question or problem. Be bold and trust the instincts you've honed through wisdom and obedience.

11. *Convert the decision into action.* Now that you've made your decision, what actions will you need to take? You won't always have a clear path or know where the decision will lead. But you can make the decision actionable by outlining your next steps.

12. *Make additions and adjustments as they come.* Taking decisive action often leads to a cascade of more decisions you'll need to make. For example, if you decide to take the new job, you'll have to decide where to live, where to go to church, how you will maintain your relationships with old friends, and so on. If you try to make all the decisions at once, you may become overwhelmed. Instead, trust that God will help you make the necessary additions and adjustments as they come.

Tips for Training Children

The Five-What Model

With practice, the 12-step model outlined above can become an intuitive process for making significant decisions. Still, it's helpful to have a stripped-down version we can teach younger children. Here is the Five-What model of decision-making.

1. What does God say?

2. What do Mom and Dad think?

3. What do I need to know?

4. What's my decision?

5. What do I do next?

Give Them Some Values-Based Practice

Decision-making is a skill developed through practice. While it's helpful for children to practice on unimportant decisions ("Would you like chicken or pizza for dinner?"), they also need opportunities to determine how to apply their values. The outcome of the decision should be substantial enough to help build their sense of responsibility. They also need to feel the choice was theirs to make, so give them a limited range of options you'd consider suitable.

Ask Your Child for Advice

A safe way to provide valuable real-world experience in decision-making is to ask them to help you think through a decision you must make. This forces them to think about a decision that is weightier than they'd normally have to consider on their own.

Ask them to use the process you taught them to think about what they would do in your situation. Take their perspective seriously and probe them about how they came up with their recommendations. Let them know that while you may not necessarily heed their advice, you take their counsel seriously and appreciate their input.

25

How to Develop Biblical Discernment

Biblical discernment is the skill of understanding and applying God's Word with the aid of the Holy Spirit to separate truth from error and right from wrong. Biblical discernment is therefore not only a habit needed to develop a biblical worldview, it is a primary reason for developing a biblical worldview. Tim Challies explains:

> The purpose of discernment is to further the chief end of man, the foremost reason we exist, which, to borrow the words of the Westminster Shorter Catechism, is "to glorify God and to enjoy him forever." By being people of discernment, we bring glory to God and learn to enjoy him ever and ever more. Conversely, if we refuse to exercise discernment and are swayed by every wind of doctrine, we deny him the glory that is rightly his and do not learn to enjoy him more.[1]

Discernment also has the practical effect of helping us to live, as John MacArthur says:

> The key to living an uncompromising life lies in one's ability to exercise discernment in every area of his or her life. For example, failure to distinguish between truth and error leaves the Christian subject to all manner of false teaching. False teaching then leads to an unbiblical mindset, which results in unfruitful and disobedient living—a certain recipe for compromise.[2]

Recognizing and rejecting false teaching is an essential element of biblical discernment—and one every Christian is expected to develop. As Paul tell us,

141

"Do not treat prophecies with contempt but test them all; hold on to what is good, reject every kind of evil" (1 Thessalonians 5:20-22).

There is much more to discernment, though, than simply avoiding false teachings, as Sinclair Ferguson explains:

> True discernment means not only distinguishing the right from the wrong; it means distinguishing the primary from the secondary, the essential from the indifferent, and the permanent from the transient. And, yes, it means distinguishing between the good and the better, and even between the better and the best.[3]

How to Develop Discernment

"How is such discernment to be obtained?" asks Ferguson. "We receive it as did Christ Himself—by the anointing of the Spirit, through our understanding of God's Word, by our experience of God's grace, and by the progressive unfolding to us of the true condition of our own hearts." Ferguson is clarifying that, as with most spiritual disciplines, biblical discernment contains both a passive and an active element. We must rely on our union with Christ and the guidance of the Holy Spirit. But we also must develop our understanding of Scripture and our ability to make critical judgments about how to apply what we learn.

Other chapters address reading and studying the Bible and how to apply it to our lives. Let's look at a few necessary steps for developing the skill of discernment:

Verify the claim. We live in a culture that veers between hyper-skepticism and gullibility. Both tend to come from a reliance on credentialed authority. For example, we tend to trust someone's opinion more if they are a celebrity or if they have "PhD" after their name. We shouldn't be dismissive of authority, but we shouldn't be cowed by it either. And when you hear a claim about what God says or what God wants, consider whether it can be verified by the Scriptures. We should be like the Berean Jews who, after hearing Paul preach, "examined the Scriptures every day to see if what Paul said was true" (Acts 17:11).

Clarify the claim. If a claim appears to be grounded in Scripture, make sure you understand the issue by seeing how Christians throughout church history have understood the issue. If the opinion of Christians is changing about certain doctrines, we should ask whether it's based on new information (a better understanding of the language or of nature that is nevertheless still consistent with Scripture) or whether it's based on what C.S. Lewis called "chronological snobbery"—the presumption that whatever has gone out of date is on that account discredited. Be particularly skeptical of claims that differ from orthodox interpretations yet align with secular culture's ever-shifting values.

Examine your instinct. What was your natural reaction on hearing the claim? "While we cannot always trust our first reactions, experience shows that God does seem to wire us in a way that our first instincts are often correct," says Tim Challies. "This is especially true when we have immersed ourselves in the Bible and have attained some level of Christian maturity."[4]

Pray for guidance. We should ask God to open our hearts to his Word and allow us to see any specific issue clearly. We should also continuously pray, as did the psalmist, "I am your servant; give me discernment" (Psalm 119:125).

Tips for Training Children

Continuous Questioning

From the time they are infants, we teach children to learn differences by asking, "Is it this or that?" They learn to discern between everything from cats and dogs to numbers and letters by noticing what distinguishes "this from that" and then putting them in a broader category.

Similarly, we teach them biblical discernment by questioning them about biblical distinctions, such as sin and mere imprudence. For example, it might not be wise to eat chocolate cake for breakfast, but it is not necessarily a sin. However, it would be a sin for a child to disobey their mother and eat cake for breakfast when they were told not to do so.

Asking questions that help children make such distinctions can help them gain a better grasp of the role of judgment in Christian liberty.

Play "Spot the Lie" in Advertising

Helping children learn to identify exaggerations or outright lies in media can help them develop their broader discernment skills. For example, ask the child to identify untruthful advertising claims. One blogger points out the advantages of this system:

It may seem silly, but actually teaching your children to pick out the lies on commercials is a really good practice in discernment. First of all, there are plenty of lies to choose from. No one's feelings get hurt, and it provides a lot of good conversation about what is truth and why the commercials are lying to you.[5]

Have Them Argue for Their Choices

When a child asks, "Why can't I?" the best answer is usually, "Because I said so." But "Why can't I?" situations can present a teaching opportunity if we force the child to make a biblical argument for their choices. For example, if a 12-year-old asks to watch an R-rated movie, you can explain what elements earned the rating (such as nudity, language, and violence) and then invite the child to make a biblically based argument for why God would approve of (or at least not object to) them watching the movie.

Teach Them to Be God-Pleasers Before People-Pleasers

Paul tells us, "Live as children of light…and find out what pleases the Lord" (Ephesians 5:8,10). Children may confuse "what pleases the Lord" with what "pleases Mom and Dad." Ideally, there won't be much difference between the two if the parents are faithful Christians. But being human, we parents tend to have biases and prejudices not wholly shared by God.

A way to help children, especially older kids, to make that distinction is to simply ask them, "What behavior or actions would you say I think are wrong but that God would not disapprove of?" Have them try to reference Scripture, though sometimes the answer will be an argument from silence (that is, the Bible doesn't say anything either for or against a behavior). And let them know you aren't going to be angry with them for honestly pointing out some examples.

PART 5

SKILLS AND HABITS FOR MENTAL AND PHYSICAL HEALTH

26

How to Sleep

The one activity we do more than any other is sleep. About one-third of each day is spent sleeping. Sleep is so essential to the functioning of our bodies that if we go too long without it, we'll die. But the importance of sleep is not limited to our physical functions—sleep is also a spiritual activity.

As John Ortberg says, "I have discovered I have a very hard time thinking and feeling and acting like Jesus when I lack sleep."[1] Sleep is a form of spiritual preparation that equips us to follow where Christ leads. Getting the rest we need is therefore one of the most important spiritual disciplines we can practice daily.

Like most spiritual disciplines, to be most effective, sleep requires both a change in attitude and a change in our practices. Here are a few steps you can take to help your child learn better sleep habits.

Maintain a Regular Sleep Schedule

One of the most important habits is to develop a regular sleep schedule. The body can't catch up on sleep, so it doesn't help letting your child sleep late on the weekends. In fact, sleeping later on some days makes it more difficult to develop a regular sleep pattern.

Get Enough Sleep

Numerous factors affect the quality of your rest, but the most important is how many hours you sleep each night. The amount of sleep a person needs varies from individual to individual and changes over the course of their lifetime.

But on average, from the ages of six to thirteen a child needs nine to eleven hours of sleep, and a teenager ages fourteen to seventeen needs between eight and ten hours a night.

Avoid Blue Light at Night

The human body has a natural clock, known as its circadian rhythm, that affects when you fall asleep and when you wake up. It's your circadian rhythm that tells your body when to produce the hormone melatonin. Melatonin levels begin to rise in mid to late evening to prepare you for sleep. The levels remain high for most of the night and then drop in the early morning hours, just before waking.

Light can disrupt melatonin levels, especially blue light, as Harvard University neuroscientist Anne-Marie Chan explains:

> Past studies have shown that light suppresses melatonin, such that light in the early evening causes a circadian delay, or resets the clock to a later schedule; and light in the early morning causes a circadian advancement, or resets the clock to an earlier schedule.[2]

Many of the devices your child is exposed to before bedtime—smartphones and tablets, laptops and televisions—are sending their eyes blue light and sending their brains the message, "Turn off the melatonin; the sun is rising, and it's time to wake up!"

The obvious fix is to have them avoid using those devices before bedtime. But if that's not always possible, use safety glasses that block blue light. They look like ordinary eyewear but block most of the light that can keep your kids awake.

Block Out Other Light Too

Unfortunately, blue light is not the only light that will affect your melatonin levels. The light coming into your child's bedroom from outside (from street lamps, car lights, the moon, and so on) can also affect their sleep. Ideally, the bedroom should be as dark as possible. Consider adding blackout curtains, shades, or drapes to their windows. Choose one that has the highest blocking potential, preferably at least 99.9 percent of light and 100 percent of UV rays.

If blackout curtains aren't an option, consider having them wear a sleep mask. The cheap ones (like you get on airplanes) are rarely comfortable or effective, so it's worth the few dollars it costs to buy one that fits properly.

If your child is afraid of the dark, look for a night-light that has a blue-free or low-blue rating. They cost about the same as regular night-lights but won't produce distracting blue light that comes from regular lightbulbs.

Limit the Caffeine

You may have been told caffeine is out of your system within 30 minutes of drinking it. That's wrong—very wrong, as Travis Bradberry explains:

> Caffeine has a six-hour half-life, which means it takes a full 24 hours to work its way out of your system. Have a cup of joe at 8 a.m., and you'll still have 25 percent of the caffeine in your body at 8 p.m. Anything you drink after noon will still be at 50 percent strength at bedtime. Any caffeine in your bloodstream—with the negative effects increasing with the dose—makes it harder to fall asleep.[3]

Keep Them Cool

When it comes to sleep, temperature matters. As a rule of thumb, you want the head to be cool (that's why you're always looking for the cool side of the pillow) and the body relatively warm.

You can usually achieve both states by setting your room temperature in the range of 65 to 70 degrees. If that sounds too cool for comfort, keep in mind that with pajamas, a sheet, and a blanket, your child's skin temperature is likely to be in the 90-degree range even if their room is only 65 degrees.[4]

How to Manage Stress

S tress is the brain's and body's response to any demand, whether emotional, mental, or physical. Because stress can affect how we feel, think, and behave, our ability to manage stress can have a profound effect on our overall outlook on life. Before we consider ways to manage stress, though, we need to develop a better understanding of what stress is and how it affects us. Here are a few realities you should know about stress.

Stress and Stressors

A stressor is anything that causes the release of stress hormones and chemicals (such as adrenaline, cortisol, and norepinephrine) that prepare the body for physical action. The two broad categories of stressors are physiological and psychological. Physiological stressors are those that put a direct demand on our body, such as injury, pain, or extreme temperatures. Psychological stressors are nonphysical demands we interpret as negative or threatening.[1] These stressors include events (being caught in a storm), situations (having to speak in public), comments (a hurtful insult from a family member), and more.

Stressors can be further divided into absolute and relative. Absolute stressors are those that would affect the bodies of nearly all people. A prime example of an absolute physical stressor is exposure to subzero temperatures, while an example of an absolute psychological stressor is being trapped in a building during a high-magnitude earthquake. Relative stressors are those that affect only some people's bodies. For example, you might become stressed about filing your tax return while a certified public accountant might have no physical reaction to the same task.[2]

Fight, Flight, or Freeze

When the stress hormones start flowing, we tend to react in one of three ways:

- Fight—a state of stress in which we feel agitated or aggressive.
- Flight—a state of stress in which we feel the urge to avoid or flee from the stressor.
- Freeze—a state of stress that causes "dysregulation," in which our energy is locked into the nervous system, causing us to freeze.[3]

Good and Bad Stress

Some stress has a negative effect on our well-being. This type is frequently referred to as "distress." But other types of stress, what psychologists call "eustress," can be helpful and even necessary for our growth. Eustress is what we feel on our wedding day or when our child is born. These bursts of stress hormones can be beneficial in that they can increase brain function, improve concentration, and boost feelings of alertness.[4]

How to Manage Stress

Your Stress and Stressors

The first step in managing stress is to identify the stressor and clarify the type of stress. Is there more than one stressor? Is it a physiological or psychological stressor? Absolute or relative? Is the stressor a temporary challenge or a long-term situation? Is a recurrent stressor causing you to have a recurring fight/flight/freeze reaction?

Take an objective view of your stress and plan your response. By taking the time to think about the stress and stressors, you can gain a modicum of control over your response. (If the stress doesn't seem to have an identifiable stressor, you may have a physiological condition, such as generalized anxiety disorder. See a doctor about how to manage such physical-based anxiety.)

Unnecessary Stressors

Sometimes the best approach to managing stress is to remove the unnecessary stressors in our life. How do we identify what is unnecessary? Ask whether the stressor can be avoided and whether it is negatively affecting your life or your relationship with God. We may be feeling stress because we are forcing ourselves to engage in behavior we'd prefer to avoid. Sinful behavior is the ultimate negative stressor, of course, and should always be avoided.

Create More Margin

If you find your stress is caused not by a single large stressor but by multiple stressors, you may need to create more margin in your life. Richard Swenson offers this explanation:

> Margin is the space between our load and our limits. It is the amount allowed beyond that which is needed. It is something held in reserve for contingencies or unanticipated situations. Margin is the gap between rest and exhaustion, the space between breathing freely and suffocating.
>
> Margin is the opposite of overload. If we are overloaded we have no margin...If we were equipped with a flashing light to indicate "100 percent full," we could better gauge our capacities. But we don't have such an indicator light, and we don't know when we have overextended until we feel the pain. As a result, many people commit to a 120 percent life and wonder why the burden feels so heavy. It is rare to see a life prescheduled to only 80 percent, leaving a margin for responding to the unexpected that God sends our way.[5]

Take Care of Your Body

"Don't you know that you yourselves are God's temple and that God's Spirit dwells in your midst?" asks Paul (1 Corinthians 3:16). We might claim to believe this verse and yet treat our bodies with less respect than we would a church building. To manage the normal and unavoidable stresses in your life, your body needs proper maintenance. You already know what to do: exercise, eat healthy, get enough sleep, drink more water, and the like. You just have to commit to doing it consistently.

Tips for Training Children

Respect Their Stress

Remember that some stressors are relative and affect people in various ways. Your child may be affected by some stressors in a completely different way than you are. For example, you may enjoy the thrill of riding roller coasters and become frustrated because your child wants to avoid them. Rather than thinking they lack courage, respect that their bodies may be conditioned to respond more strongly and more negatively than your own does. (And while you want to raise a courageous child, they should be taught true courage involves actions such as standing up for others, not sitting on a ride at an amusement park.)

Help Identify Stress and Stressors

By teaching your child how stress works and the types of stress they can expect, you can help them understand that what they are dealing with is natural and often manageable. Giving children appropriate labels for their stressors helps you communicate with them about their stress. Eventually, you'll be able to ask, "What stressors at school are affecting you?"

Shield Them from Your Stress

We don't need to present a false front to our children or give them the impression we live a stress-free life. But we should frequently shield children from our stressors. While we may wish we too could be shielded from financial problems or troubles at work, we have something the child doesn't have—a modicum of control over the situation. Exposing children to stressful situations they cannot control can cause unnecessary anxiety.

Unstructured Play

"Free play" is self-directed and an end in itself rather than part of an organized activity. Children need this type of play for their emotional and cognitive development, and yet they often don't get enough. "Since about 1955...children's free play has been continually declining, at least partly because adults have exerted ever-increasing control over children's activities," says Peter Gray, a former professor of psychology at Boston College.[6]

Research has found that children spent less time in play and had less free time in 1997 than they did in 1981. They spent 18 percent more time at school, 145 percent more time doing schoolwork, and 168 percent more time shopping with parents. The researchers found that children in 1997 spent only about 11 hours per week at play (including computer play). Now consider how much has changed since 1997. Does your own child get 11 hours of free play per week?

Ensuring your child gets enough free play—especially play that includes physical activity—is essential in helping them manage their stress.

Box Breathing

One of the most common physiological reactions to stress is shallow breathing or holding our breath. Our brains get less oxygen, which heightens our anxiety and impedes our ability to respond. Fortunately, you can teach your child a simple breathing technique so powerful Navy SEALs use it to help them react in combat situations.

The technique is called box breathing (also known as four-square breathing or square-box breathing) and combines deep breathing with simple counting. Here's how it works:

> First, inhale your breath slowly for a count of four. Then, hold the breath for an equal count of four. Release the breath all the way out through pursed lips, on a count of four. Finally, wait four seconds before saying or doing anything. Repeat the cycle a few more times or as long as you need to help you relax. Always breathe from the lower belly instead of from the upper chest. It may help you to place one or both of your hands on your abdomen or sides to feel the lower part of your abdomen rise as you breathe in.[7]

Have children practice the box breathing technique when they are relaxed so they will be prepared to apply it when they find themselves in stressful situations.

How to Handle Loss and Grief

Grief is the normal and natural emotional reaction to loss or to a change in a familiar pattern of behavior.[1] We tend to associate grief with the loss of a loved one, but the emotion may arise with any significant change in our life, such as divorce or moving to a new city. Because we live in a world of painful change—some caused by sin and death—we and our children will inevitably face loss and grief.

Grief is a universal emotion that humans have experienced throughout history, but our union with Christ should lead us to deal with grief in unique ways. Here are a few things we should remember when we grieve.

We grieve with God. When Jesus saw Mary weeping over the death of her brother, Lazarus, he was "deeply moved in spirit and troubled" and began to weep himself (John 11:33-35). Even though Jesus knew he would soon be bringing Lazarus back from the dead, he was overcome with the emotion of losing his friend. When we experience loss, we should take comfort in knowing God mourns and grieves with us.

We grieve with other believers. We are united with Christ, and he is united with other members of his church, so we are united to these other believers through him. This is not a mere symbolic unity, but a deep, spiritual reality. We can grieve knowing others share in our grief, even if the loss was not their own. We can truly "mourn with those who mourn" (Romans 12:15) because of the unbreakable connection we believers share through Jesus.

We grieve with hope. "The Bible does not dismiss or minimize grief, and we shouldn't underestimate its impact," says Elizabeth Groves. "But we grieve differently than those without hope."[2] As Paul says, "Brothers and sisters, we do not want you to be uninformed about those who sleep in death, so that you do not grieve like the rest of mankind, who have no hope. For we believe that Jesus died and rose again, and so we believe that God will bring with Jesus those who have fallen asleep in him" (1 Thessalonians 4:13-14).

Tips for Training Children

Know What to Expect

Every child responds to grief differently, but Claudia L. Jarrett has identified three "phases of grief" children often go through after a loss: early grief, acute grief, and integration of loss and grief.

Early grief includes such reactions in children as shock and numbing, alarm, denial, and hyperactivity. Acute grief often manifests in such behaviors as yearning, pining, and searching (including looking to the past); expressing strong emotions, such as anger or sadness; disorganization or disorientation; and despair or depression. The last stage, integration of loss and grief, involves talking about the loss, getting involved again in enjoyable activities, and showing concern and care toward others.[3]

Telling a Child About Death

"Children old enough to love are old enough to grieve," says Christian social worker Jeanine Bozeman. "Adults need to be aware that grief is a normal emotional response to death." Bozeman offers suggestions for how we can tell a child about the death of a loved one.

- Talk to the child as soon as possible after the death.
- Give the child a simple, honest explanation using clear, concise words.
- Talk with the child in familiar surroundings.
- Be sure the child understands the meanings of your words.
- Give adequate but not detailed information about the death.
- Address the child's fears and anxieties.

- Reassure the child he or she is not to blame for the death and that someone will care for him.
- Listen carefully to the child, validating feelings, assisting with overwhelming feelings, and involving and including him.
- Continue the child's routine.
- Model appropriate grief behaviors.
- Provide opportunities to remember the loved one who has died.[4]

Provide Boundaries

You might be tempted to excuse certain behaviors because the child is suffering loss. But they need boundaries and guidance in how to express their emotions in a healthy way. If you allow a child to be violent or emotionally manipulative while grieving, they'll believe they can carry on such actions later.

Let them know which types of behavior are natural and acceptable (such as crying and being upset and sad) and which will not be tolerated (hitting siblings, frequently lashing out at parents and teachers, and so on).

Your Grief and Their Grief

If you lose someone you love, such as your own parent, you might be shocked and frustrated by what appears to be a lack of observed grief by your child. They may show a stronger emotional reaction to the loss of a family pet than to their own grandparent. This may seem callous or unloving, but it may be a natural reaction. Remember that the emotion of grief is deeply connected to a change in a familiar pattern of behavior.

Your deep sense of grief is likely connected to the loss of someone who has been in your life for decades and with whom you once had frequent, even daily interactions. But your child may not have as deep a connection, especially if the death is of a relative whom they only saw infrequently. This is why the death of a pet—which is in their life every day—may invoke a stronger emotional reaction. Be gracious and patient and give them space to grieve in their own way.

How to Deal with Fear and Anxiety

O f all the major characters in the Bible, who was the most prone to anxiety and fear? If we judge by how often they expressed their fears and anxieties, the answer must be King David. Fear and anxiety were his constant companions. They are also primary themes of the psalms. As he wrote in Psalm 139, "Search me, God, and know my heart; test me and know my anxious thoughts" (verse 23).

David had a lot of reasons to be anxious and afraid. While still a young man, he faced down bears, lions, and an enormous Philistine warrior. Throughout his life, innumerable and merciless enemies sought to destroy him. His mentor, King Saul, tried to kill him, as did his own son Absalom. He lived in nearly constant danger. Yet in Psalm 34 we see where David found solace:

> I sought the Lord, and he answered me;
> > he delivered me from all my fears (verse 4).
> The angel of the Lord encamps around those who fear him,
> > and he delivers them (verse 7).
> Fear the Lord, you his holy people,
> > for those who fear him lack nothing (verse 9).
> Come, my children, listen to me;
> > I will teach you the fear of the Lord (verse 11).

How did David find comfort and protection from fear and yet fear the Lord? Before we can answer the question, we must first understand what we mean by fear and anxiety and the different meanings of the term "fear."

Fear and Anxiety

Anxiety and fear are similar emotions working on different time frames. Fear is an emotional response to a real or perceived *immediate* threat; anxiety is an emotional response to a real or perceived *future* threat. Fear is a physiological and/or emotional warning system that alerts us to danger right now, while anxiety is a warning system of impending danger.

Depending on the context, fear and anxiety may be God-given capacities for survival, or they may be sinful responses to God's providential care. For instance, the Bible frequently tells us we should have a reverential fear of God. And if confronted with an immediate threat to our life—such as encountering a dangerous animal—we should be respectfully fearful enough to flee for our own safety and survival.

Regarding anxiety, Paul says, "I want you to be free from anxieties. The unmarried man is anxious about the things of the Lord, how to please the Lord. But the married man is anxious about worldly things, how to please his wife, and his interests are divided" (1 Corinthians 7:32-34 ESV). He seems to imply such "anxieties" (other translations use the word "concerns") are not inherently sinful.

Note that in such cases we are referring to fear and anxiety that are both occasional and contextual to normal life. For some people, anxiety is a physiological malfunction that has become both disordered and debilitating. If you or your child suffers from persistent anxious thoughts on most days of the week for six months, if the anxiety interferes with daily functioning, and if you have anxiety-related symptoms (such as trouble sleeping), you may have a medical condition such as generalized anxiety disorder, panic disorder, or social anxiety. In such cases you should seek help from a counselor or physician. This chapter does not refer to those conditions and refers only to the anxiety and fear we have control over.

Two Types of Fear

In Psalm 34, David says he was delivered from all his fears and yet says he will teach "the fear of the LORD" (verse 11). What does he mean by that? David is referring to two types of fears: *filial* fear and *servile* fear. Philipp Melanchthon, a collaborator with Martin Luther, discusses what it means to fear God by contrasting these two fears.

Filial fear is the type of respect and love a child has for a parent, a fear of offending the one they most adore and trust. In contrast, servile fear is the kind of fear a prisoner has for his jailor or executioner.[1] Filial fear, says Melanchthon, includes faith, while servile fear is without faith:

> Servile fear is a dread without faith and it actually runs away from God; but filial fear is a dread to which faith has been added, which steers between these two kinds of dread and comforts the heart and approaches God, prays for and receives remission.[2]

David's faith led him to have a *filial* fear of the Lord. In turn, the Lord delivered David from the *servile* fear of his enemies.

The Uncomfortable Truth

Now that we've clarified the meaning of the terms, we must face an uncomfortable reality: Much of our fear and anxiety is sinful, for it reveals we lack trust in God. Anxiety may be an appropriate emotion if it provokes us to obey God. For instance, if we fear our marriage will fall apart because we have been neglecting our spouse, we should take necessary steps to reconcile. Similarly, we should avoid or remove ourselves from situations that are needlessly and recklessly dangerous or imperiling. For example, a father may be justified in putting his life in danger while serving God in a mission field, but he may be acting foolishly and risking making orphans of his children for the sake of an adrenaline rush by engaging in dangerous hobbies.

Overcoming Fear and Anxiety

David shows us how to overcome fear and anxiety—by seeking God. Nothing else will work. No shortcuts or exercises can shore up our courage or calm our faithless heart. Stephen J. Cole highlights the wisdom behind this truth:

> We don't have here a simple formula for overcoming fear. What we have is a way of life: Seeking the Lord is the way to overcome fear. If God gave us a formula, we'd use it and then forget God until the next crisis. But seeking the Lord is a daily matter.

When our children are afraid they seek us, their parents, for comfort and protection. We too should seek God with a childlike faith that he will protect and comfort us from what scares us. Even if we are not immediately delivered, even if we must face the source of our fear, by standing with God we can know peace. When we are captivated by a vision of the beauty, majesty, and sovereignty of God, the evils and dangers of this world will appear small in comparison.[3]

Tips for Training Children

Distinguish Between Servile Fear and Filial Fear

This can be a difficult distinction for adults to understand, so we have to make a special effort to explain it in a way a child can grasp. This is the key difference: Servile fear arises because we fear an injustice or harm will be done to us, while filial fear comes from love and respect. We should be somewhat frightened by an authority (including a parent or God) who loves us but who also may have to punish our wrongdoing or correct our misbehavior.

One of the best ways to help children understand this concept is to read to them C.S. Lewis's Narnia Chronicles. Throughout the novels the characters have a filial fear of Aslan. Consider, for example, this exchange from *The Lion, the Witch, and the Wardrobe*:

> "Aslan is a lion—the Lion, the great Lion."
> "Ooh" said Susan. "I'd thought he was a man. Is he—quite safe? I shall feel rather nervous about meeting a lion…"
> "Safe?" said Mr Beaver…"Who said anything about safe? 'Course he isn't safe. But he's good. He's the King, I tell you."

Don't Scare Your Kids

This is directed toward fathers. As thousands of online videos show, many fathers seem to enjoy pranks that frighten their children. I'm sure well-meaning dads can think of dozens of reasons to keep doing them, but here's an important reason not to: They undermine the distinction between filial fear and servile fear.

We fathers are called to model our heavenly Father. We are tasked with protecting and comforting our children and making sure they feel safe—at least in our presence. When our lame attempts at humor frighten our kids, we make them feel unsafe and insecure. We may also be planting a seed of doubt that their heavenly Father will keep them safe. So leave the scary pranks to their friends and siblings, and keep your focus on being their security and protector.

Identify the Source of a Child's Anxiety

You can help prepare yourself to deal with the anxieties of older children by having them fill in the blanks in the following sentences:

What I need most is _____.

What I want most is _____.

What I most want to avoid is _____.

What I'm most concerned about in life is _____.

What I feel most powerless about is _____.

The answers to those questions will likely reveal their sources of anxiety.[4] We tend to feel anxious when think we won't get what we need or want—or that we'll get what we don't want or can't avoid. We also become anxious about concerns that make us feel small, helpless, or lacking control. By uncovering the potential areas of anxiety, you'll be better able to address the child's concerns.

Five Ways to Help Your Child Fight Fear

Leslie Schmucker, a retired school teacher, offers five ways to help your child fight their fear:

1. *Listen.* "This is not the time to offer advice," says Schmucker. "Just let them talk, and make sure they know that you have heard them."

2. *Acknowledge their fear.* "While you are acknowledging the fear, don't give it credence. Help them to see that God is bigger. Teach your children to push through it, facing the fear head on. Don't resist it. Rather, ride it out. It will pass," says Schmucker.

3. *Keep perspective, and keep moving.* "Remind your children their enemy is 'the father of lies' (John 8:44), and that their heavenly Father is the only one whose voice is worth listening to," says Schmucker. "Teach your children that their strength comes from Christ, while fear is from the enemy (2 Timothy 1:7)."

4. *Pray with your child, rehearsing God's Word.* "When your children start to

feel anxious, stop everything and pray with them. This is a golden opportunity to help them realize the importance of prayer." Schmucker recommends committing to memory helpful Scripture verses such as Zephaniah 3:17; Philippians 4:6; and 1 Peter 5:7.

5. *Keep Christ at the center.* Parents may want to let their child retreat from anxiety-producing situations, such as school activities, as a way of protecting their child. But Schmucker suggests switching the focus:

> Modern culture places children square at the center of the universe—both their own and everyone else's. But this is not biblical. Our children must be taught that Christ is the center, that everything we do must glorify him, and that in doing so, we will be given great joy and peace. When we model for our children confidence in Christ (as opposed to modeling a spirit of fear and self-focus), we are training them up in the way they should go (Proverbs 22:6).
>
> Being allowed to exit life (staying home from school, isolating from friends, ceasing all activity) in response to anxiety is, I feel, an error too many parents make. It has been my daughter's and my experience that when we stay in the game, focusing on Christ and telling ourselves the truth, we come out the other side stronger, more resilient, and closer to our only Source of peace.

How to Develop a Healthy Body Image

Body image is the mental representation we create of what we think we look like, which may or may not be the way others see us. Many children, both girls and boys, struggle with a negative body image.

For girls, negative body images are often associated with a desire to be thin. By age six, girls start to express concerns about their own weight or shape, and 40 to 60 percent of elementary school girls (ages six to twelve) are concerned about their weight or about becoming too fat.[1] In contrast, boys tend to feel pressure to gain weight. "There are some males who do want to be thinner and are focused on thinness," says Dr. Alison Field, an associate professor of pediatrics at Boston Children's Hospital, "but many more are focused on wanting bigger or at least more toned and defined muscles. That's a very different physique."[2]

For both boys and girls, the problem often stems from a desire to conform to the physical standards set by media and advertising. According to the Centers for Disease Control, the average height for women in America age twenty and older is 5 feet 3 inches, and the average weight is 168.5 pounds.[3] For fashion models the average is 5 feet 10 inches and 120 pounds.[4] For boys, the dissatisfaction is most often with having well-developed muscles. Research suggests that exposure to media's ideal of muscularity, and not muscularity per se, elicits body dissatisfaction in men with preexisting muscularity concerns.[5]

While media and advertising have a significant impact on body image, research has shown religious beliefs can provide a healthy counterbalance.

A study published in the *Journal of Religion and Health* found that people who hold a religious belief that considers the body to be "sanctified" (holy, worthy of respect, and integral to one's being) are significantly more likely to have a positive and healthy image of their bodies, while those who consider the body shameful were more likely to have a negative image of their bodies.[6] "The belief that one's body is 'just something I live in here on earth,' the belief that one's body is sinful and meant to be subdued, and [the belief] that one's body is less important to God than one's soul were linked to body shame," note the researchers. "In contrast, beliefs reflecting Christian teachings that one's body is a temple of God, created specifically by God, and that God is glorified and honored through one's body, were linked to appreciating one's body."

Tips for Training Children

Know What God Says

The challenge for parents is to help children exchange the world's view of their bodies for a mental representation of how God wants us to see our bodies. The most effective way to help children develop a healthy body image is to have their own perceptions be rooted in Scripture. Here are eight Bible passages that should serve as the foundation of how your child should think of their bodies: Genesis 1:26-27; 1 Samuel 16:7; Psalm 139:14; Matthew 23:27; Luke 16:15; 2 Corinthians 4:16; Ephesians 2:10; 1 Peter 3:3-4.

Be Gracious and Realistic

We need to present a scriptural view of our bodies in a way that avoids condescending clichés ("Everyone is beautiful in their own way") and trite truisms ("It's what's on the inside that counts"). Focus instead on being positive but realistic. Learning to love our bodies is a lifelong process. Even as your child makes advances in gaining a healthy body image, they will have setbacks and failures. Show them grace throughout the process.

Everyone Is Insecure

The lie that we are not worthy of love because we have physical flaws is whispered by Satan into the ears of every human. Your child can take comfort in knowing they are not alone and that everyone struggles with body-image issues. But more importantly, this realization should motivate them to reach out to others in love, knowing they are going through the same trials.

Be Their Body-Image Model

The most important way you can help your child develop a healthy body image is to be an example. "We will not teach our children to love and embrace their God-given selves if we fail to model it for them," says Sharon Hodde Miller. "How we treat our bodies, change our bodies, and talk about our bodies will impact how our children view their own bodies."[7]

PART 6

SKILLS AND HABITS FOR CHARACTER DEVELOPMENT

How to Develop Godly Grit

What characteristic in children is the most significant predictor of worldly success? Intelligence? Talent? Attractiveness? After years of research, psychologist Angela Lee Duckworth discovered it wasn't any of those. It was grit.

> Grit is passion and perseverance for very long-term goals. Grit is having stamina. Grit is sticking with your future, day in, day out, not just for the week, not just for the month, but for years, and working really hard to make that future a reality. Grit is living life like it's a marathon, not a sprint.[1]

Grit is also one of the most important character traits for spiritual formation. If you want your children to become like Jesus, they need to develop godly grit.[2]

The Bible's terms for grit are "steadfastness" and "endurance."[3] Steadfastness is the determination, as Paul says, to stand firm and refuse to let anything move you from your goal (1 Corinthians 15:58). It is the resolve to keep working for the Lord no matter what trials may come. Endurance is the determination to keep moving toward your goal despite external challenges and internal weariness (Luke 21:19).

Godly grit is a trait, empowered by God's grace, that we acquire through standing firm in the face of challenges and adversity.

Tips for Training Children

Help Them Identify Spiritual Goals

You can't develop passion and perseverance for achieving long-term spiritual goals if you don't have a clear understanding of what those goals are. Have your child write down a list of their goals, including five ways in which they want to become more like Jesus.

Rely on Routine

The more your child can rely on habits and established routines to guide their spiritual formation, the less they have to rely on pure perseverance to move them toward their goals.

Teach Them to Expect Hardship

Your child will be better prepared to stand firm in the face of adversity if they are mentally, physically, and spiritually prepared for the hardships that will come (and hardships *will* come).

Teach Them to Emulate "Gritty" People

Noah, Abraham, Joseph, Paul…the Bible is filled with examples of people who had grit. Their stories have much to teach us about perseverance and endurance (Romans 15:4).

Don't Tell Your Kid They Are Smart

This may sound counterintuitive, but if you want to raise an intelligent child, don't praise them for their intelligence. Kids will get the impression intelligence is a fixed attribute they possess rather than an aptitude that can grow during their lifetime. James Hamblin offers this explanation:

> The idea is that when we praise kids for being smart, those kids think: *Oh good, I'm smart.* And then later, when those kids mess up, which they will, they think: *Oh no, I'm not smart after all. People will think I'm not smart after all.* And that's the worst. That's a risk to avoid, they learn. "Smart" kids stand to become especially averse to making mistakes, which are critical to learning and succeeding.[4]

Instead of praising them for being smart, praise them for their grit. Show them what matters most is sustained effort and hard work rather than a natural intellectual aptitude.

Let Them Fail

Failure is a road sign, as C.S. Lewis said, that directs us toward achievement. If we are too afraid to let our child fail—in areas both big and small—we prevent them from developing the grit they need to achieve. Take the bubble wrap off your kids and let them take risks. Don't be surprised when they fail (that is to be expected), but be prepared to help them work through their failures. Be ready to coach and encourage them to pick themselves up and try again.

32

How to Tame Your Tongue

Taming is a process by which a wild beast is subdued into adapting and submitting to human control. James, the brother of Jesus, observes, "All kinds of animals, birds, reptiles and sea creatures are being tamed and have been tamed by mankind" (James 3:7). But despite mankind's success in taming the animal kingdom, James mentions one wild thing we haven't been able to subdue and adapt: "No human being can tame the tongue" (verse 8).

While we may never fully tame our tongues, we can—with the help of the Holy Spirit—take steps to make our words more edifying and more like Jesus. None of these steps will be new, for every believer who has read the Bible has been instructed on taming our tongues. But as the famed English writer Samuel Johnson once said, "People need to be reminded more often than they need to be instructed." So here are a few reminders of how we can be more careful with our words.

Look to Your Union with Christ

The expression "in Christ" occurs 216 times in the letters of Paul and 26 times in the writings of John. The word "in" is the connective hinge of the doctrine referred to as "union with Christ." Union with Christ means you are in Christ and Christ is in you.

Because we are united to him, Jesus gives us the power and ability to do whatever he requires of us. Because of this union with Christ, we can say, as Paul does, "I can do all things through him who strengthens me" (Philippians

4:13 ESV). We are better able to understand we can change when we remember our union with Christ—that Jesus is in us and helping us tame our tongues.

Consider Silence

Almost every action movie includes a scene where the villain captures the hero. Our hero's hands and feet are bound, or he is being held at gunpoint or is in some way helpless and at the mercy of the villain. And every time the hero insults or provokes the villain, resulting in physical punishment. We may admire the hero's resolve, but we tend to think, "Why didn't they just keep their mouth shut?"

We're acknowledging that the hero had a choice not to say anything. Yet we often forget we have the same choice. The book of Proverbs tells us, "Those who guard their lips preserve their lives, but those who speak rashly will come to ruin" (13:3), and "Those who guard their mouths and their tongues keep themselves from calamity" (21:23).

Oftentimes we won't suffer a physical beating for what we say. More likely, our words will be used to hurt others. But we can spare ourselves and others a lot of pain by simply recognizing we don't have to verbalize everything we think.

Understand Why You Talk

Proverbs also tells us, "Even fools are thought wise if they keep silent, and discerning if they hold their tongues" (17:28). Why do we refuse to be silent, even when that would be to our benefit? Often we refuse to remain silent because we believe we are engaged in zero-sum verbal exchanges. If we refuse to speak, the other person will win.

But in reality, we rarely win in such situations. We don't change the other person's mind or make them think more highly of us. All we gain is the fleeting emotional high of delivering a stinging rebuke. We don't recognize that we are trading a temporary buzz for the permanent benefit of being thought wise and discerning.

Seek to Understand Before Responding

In his classic bestseller *7 Habits of Highly Effective People*, Stephen R. Covey says a key to effective communication is to "seek first to understand, then to be understood."

If you're like most people, you probably seek first to be understood; you want to get your point across. And in doing so, you may ignore the other person completely, pretend that you're listening, selectively hear only certain parts of the conversation or attentively focus on only the words being said, but miss the meaning entirely. So why does this happen? Because most people listen with the intent to reply, not to understand. You listen to yourself as you prepare in your mind what you are going to say, the questions you are going to ask, etc.[1]

The solution is simply to listen. Only by truly listening can we understand both what someone is saying and how we should respond. As Proverbs says, "To answer before listening—that is folly and shame" (18:13).

Be Slow to Speak Your Mind

Imagine your next thought being heard by hundreds or even thousands of people and then shared with millions. For most of human history, that ability was limited to only a handful of the most influential people on the planet. Yet today, because of communication tools like social media, our every utterance—whether silly or profound, wise or foolish—can be sent across the globe.

Such power should make us extremely cautious about what we say or write. And yet we tend to be less careful about what we say than ever before. The immediate gratification that comes from instant communication entices us to be quick to speak our mind—often before we've measured our words.

The Bible is clear such behavior is foolish. "Do you see someone who speaks in haste?" asks Proverbs 29:20. "There is more hope for a fool than for them." How then can we be less hasty? One way is to set a time limit before you speak or write on a public platform. If the thought once seemed witty or funny but isn't worth saying after a cool-down period of a few hours or few days, then maybe it wasn't as interesting as you thought.

Avoid Profanity—Build Up Others

We live in a culture where profanity and obscene remarks have become commonplace. Falling into this trap can be easy even for believers. But the Bible sets a higher standard. "Do not let any unwholesome talk come out of your mouths, but only what is helpful for building others up according to their needs, that it may benefit those who listen" (Ephesians 4:29).

Remember We Are Accountable

Perhaps the most effective means of taming our tongue is reminding ourselves God will hold us responsible for every ungodly remark we make. Every one. As Jesus says, "I tell you that everyone will have to give account on the day of judgment for every empty word they have spoken" (Matthew 12:36). When we believe this is true, taming our tongues is much easier.

Tips for Training Children

Teach Them What the Bible Says

Children aren't likely to know what the Bible says about managing our speech unless we tell them. This may seem obvious, but it's an area of teaching we often overlook. Children are more likely to assume it's their parents, rather than God, who are telling them to watch their mouth. Help them memorize some of the verses listed above so the topic is embedded in their hearts.

Show Them a Better Way

When correcting a child for speaking foolishly, show them what they should say instead. Sometimes, of course, what they should have said is nothing at all. Find ways to praise them for holding their tongue when you recognize they are tempted to say something they shouldn't.

Be Consistent About the Standard

Children see parents laughing at obscenities but are told not to repeat "adult language." Then they see their parents laughing at profanities uttered by a toddler and are told not to repeat such words because babies don't know what they're saying. Children learn that nothing is inherently wrong with such vulgar talk and that an inexplicable and inconsistent age-based standard applies to such language. If we want them to believe God disapproves of such unwholesome talk, we must be consistent in our denunciation of vulgar language.

Exemplify Repentance

When our children catch us using unwholesome talk and call us out, we should accept the rebuke as if it came from any other follower of Christ. We may need to correct the *way* they corrected us, but we should model repentance and humility.

Apologize for not only failing to meet the biblical standard but also for not setting the proper example for them. By acknowledging our words have dishonored God, we show our children how seriously they should approach the task of taming their own tongues.

33

How to Develop Virtuous Habits

Imagine an alien from another solar system comes to Earth to learn as much about you as possible and predict your future behavior. The alien doesn't want you to be aware of its presence, so it cannot contact you directly. It has only seven days to submit a report to its superiors. What would be the most effective means for it to complete its task?

The obvious answer is to simply observe your behavior. Are you punctual in meeting the demands of your job, or are you unreliable? Do you go for a walk every day or eat an entire box of cookies every night? Do you spend hours watching television or spend your free time reading?

The alien may not know everything about you, but it will have learned more than you might imagine since, as the historian Will Durant says, "We are what we repeatedly do." In other words, we are (largely) the sum of our habits.

A habit is a recurrent, often unconscious pattern of behavior acquired through frequent repetition. Habits, whether good or bad, are behavior or practices that have become so ingrained they are often done without conscious thought. Why do you turn on the television every night at 8 p.m.? Why do you shower before brushing your teeth? Why do you follow the same route to work every day? Throughout our day we reenact patterns of behavior that have become so ingrained in our daily routine we don't even think about them.

Habits drive our behavior, which in turn forms our character. No one wakes up one day to find they've suddenly developed an immoral character or a godly one. Through habits of rebelliousness against God, we become "slaves to sin." Through habits of obedience and obeying from our heart the "pattern of teaching that has now claimed [our] allegiance," we become "slaves to righteousness" (Romans 6:15-18).

Our character is shaped by the responses we make to thousands of decisions over the course of our lives. Most of the time we respond without consciously thinking about how to act. We tell the truth because we've made a habit of doing so. Over time we become honest and trustworthy because the habit of telling the truth has become ingrained in our character.

Five general types of habits are related to character development: neutral, virtuous, positive, negative, and sinful. Neutral habits are those that have no detectable influence on our character (such as which route you take to work). Positive habits improve our lives in a general way (for example, brushing our teeth), while virtuous habits are those that help form us into Christlikeness (including prayer and Scripture reading). Negative habits have generally adverse effects on our life (such as eating too much junk food), while sinful habits are those that lead us away from God and to our destruction.

Because of the special role virtuous habits play in character development, we need to understand how they work, how they're formed, and how positive habits can be created.

How Habits Work

Habits emerge because the brain is constantly looking for ways to save effort. God designed our brains to automate mundane and rote tasks (such as walking) so we might have more mental energy to spend on spiritual or cultural tasks (such as worship or creating art).

Every habit starts with a behavioral pattern called a "habit loop," which consists of a cue, a routine, and a reward. The cue is a type of trigger that tells your brain to enter automatic mode and begin the routine, which is the behavior itself. The final step is the reward—an internal or external stimulus that satisfies your brain and helps it remember the habit loop.

Consider, for example, one of the most frequently practiced habits of personal hygiene. As you prepare to go to bed at night (the cue), your brain reminds you to brush your teeth (the routine). The fresh, clean feeling that results provides a positive experience (the reward).

If you forget to follow this routine, you may find your brain sending you a reminder or a signal something is wrong (usually after you're comfortably warm and snug in bed). This is because habits satisfy a neurological craving—our brains look forward to the sense of fulfillment that comes with completing the routine. This is also why it becomes so hard to not check our email when we receive a notification. Even if we know the email is something that can be handled later, our brains want us to close the loop by completing our habitual routine.[1]

Tips for Training Children

Creating new virtuous habits requires applying the following four steps.

Identify the Habit Loop

The new pattern of behavior you want to create will consist of the habit loop—a cue, a routine, and a reward. Take a few minutes to think through and write down the details of each part of the loop. For example, let's use the habit of daily Bible reading. To set up the routine—the main action of the habit, such as reading a passage of Scripture—we'll need to identify the materials needed (access to a Bible and a quiet place to read) and establish a time to consistently carry out the habit loop. The more you understand the habit loop you are creating, the easier it will be to identify problems that might prevent the process from becoming a habitual behavior.

Isolate the Cue

Cues are signals that tell us to begin the habit routine. In his book *The Power of Habit*, Charles Duhigg says research has shown that almost all habitual cues fit into one of five categories: location, time, emotional state, other people, and immediately preceding action.[2] To create a habit loop, choose a cue that takes advantage of as many of these categories as possible. For instance, our cue could be walking into our bedroom (location and immediately preceding action) at 8 p.m. (time) when the kids have been put to bed (other people) and we are relieved to have a few moments to ourselves (emotional state).

Create a Reward

When creating a virtuous habit, pinpointing a reward can be difficult. Why should we reward ourselves or our children for doing something we should do anyway? And isn't the virtuous habit a reward in itself?

Many people feel guilty or frustrated about creating a reward for a good habit. This is understandable. But keep in mind you are not rewarding yourself or your child for doing the right thing; you're training the brain to create a neurological craving. A reward (such as eating a small piece of candy) for reading a devotional isn't an incentive or a prize. It's merely a way to control the way our brain responds to the habit loop.

Plan and Evaluate

Habits are difficult to consciously create because they have not yet become unconscious, scripted behaviors. The conscious part—making sure your brain is actively focused on the habit loop—is the stumbling block. For the habit loop to become an ingrained habit requires effort and persistence. You need a plan that outlines how you'll handle obstacles and what you'll do when you miss the schedule and need to get back on track. Similarly, you'll need to continuously evaluate the habit loop to ensure you have effective cues and rewards.

How to Change Negative Habits

Negative habits have adverse effects on our life, while sinful habits lead us away from God and to our destruction. All sinful habits are ultimately negative, but not all negative habits are sinful. This distinction is not trivial. Parents have the authority to determine what habits are negative, but only God has the right to determine what is sinful.

Consider, for example, the well-intentioned but wholly unscriptural maxim that cleanliness is next to godliness. The adage is so established, John Wesley said in a sermon in 1791 that "cleanliness is, indeed, next to godliness," and "slovenliness is no part of religion."[1] Wesley and others would presumably agree that while slovenliness has a negative impact on our lives, it is not inherently a sin against God. Yet how many children have heard that claim and assumed that failing to maintain certain standards of hygiene is some form of sin?

When teaching children, we must always be careful not to let them be confused between what we prefer and what God commands.

Still, God has given parents the responsibility to train children in behavior that will lead to their flourishing (Proverbs 22:6). We can use our prudential judgment to determine what habits will have a negative effect on their lives and help them overcome such habits.

Identify Negative Habits

Just as negative habits can sometimes be mistaken for sinful habits, they can also be mistaken for neutral habits. While we may think a pattern of behavior is having no ill effect on our life, our friends and family may disagree. For example, we may enjoy staying up late on the weekends so we can be alone. This may not necessarily be a negative habit, but it could be causing us to get an inadequate amount of sleep or lead us to sleep late instead of spending time with friends and family. Because our behavior affects others, we should ask those closest to us for input on what they consider to be our negative habits.

Make a list of all the patterns of behavior you are unsure about. Do the habits on your list prevent you from serving God and your neighbor? Do some habits have long-term effects that may not be causing problems for you now but could affect you later in life? Are there habits on your list that you criticize when you see them in the lives of your children? Be brutally honest in assessing your behavior and commit to eventually changing every negative habit on the list.

Isolate the Habit Loop

Every habit, whether positive or negative, starts with a "habit loop." As we discussed in chapter 33, this loop consists of three parts: a cue, a routine, and a reward. The cue is a type of trigger that tells your brain to enter automatic mode and begin the routine, which is the behavior itself. The final step is the reward—an internal or external stimulus that satisfies your brain and helps it remember the habit loop.

Change the Trigger

You can overcome some negative habits simply by changing the trigger. For example, consider the negative habit of checking your email when you are trying to engage in another activity, such as Bible reading. The cue for this habit is likely a notification (visual or audio) that you have a new email. This triggers the behavior (checking your email) your brain has been conditioned to reward (the brain likes novelty, and reading an email temporarily satisfies our curiosity). By simply turning off such notifications we can remove the trigger that activates the behavior.

Modify the Context

Along with the three parts of the habit loop, negative habits tend to include a strong contextual element. Specifically, we are more likely to engage in negative habits when we are bored, stressed, or seeking to avoid an activity (as when we procrastinate working).

Replace the Negative Habit with a Positive One

Eliminating a negative habit is extremely difficult. But the process can be much easier if we replace the habit with a better one. Once you've identified the negative habit, consider how you can reengineer the habit loop to replace it with a more positive routine.

Plan for Setbacks

Negative habits are difficult to overcome. Expect to make numerous attempts and experience lots of trial and error before you're able to replace a negative habit with one that aids in your flourishing. Ask God to give you the strength and ability to persevere.

Tips for Training Children

Identify the Trigger

The first step to helping your child change a negative habit is to understand why they engage in the behavior. Many, if not most, negative habits are developed because of a lack of control. Children, especially younger children, do not have much direct control over their own lives. They don't often get to make decisions adults would consider trivial, such as what they will eat or when they go to bed. This can lead to a range of negative emotions, from frustration to fear.

Children often develop negative habits as coping mechanisms for such emotions. For example, infants learn early on that sucking their thumb or finger has a comforting effect. Toddlers who revert to that behavior may be attempting to comfort themselves because of a new stressor in their lives. Knowing why they are engaging in the habit can help us not only change the behavior but help the child cope with a difficulty they may be having.

Modify the Context

Kids eventually outgrow certain habits. The most obvious is picking their nose and then eating the contents. Adults naturally consider this repulsive. We may also fear other people will see our children doing this (Spoiler alert: Most other kids your child's age do it too), and so we try to end the habit by fiat. The problem is, the benefits of nose-picking are difficult for children to pass up.

A better approach would be to give them a two-prong solution. First, help them understand why you consider the behavior to be harmful. You could explain to them in terms they'd understand how germs cause sickness and mucous is the body's way of getting rid of the bad germs. By their eating their boogers, they are simply putting the bad germs back into their bodies. Second, help them find a better way to get the same benefits. For example, you can show them how to put a tissue over their finger to clear their nose. Then, rather than eating the boogers, they can examine the contents of the tissue to admire their efforts at expelling sickness-causing germs.

Yes, looking at snot is gross—but not as gross as eating it. Sometimes the best way to change a negative habit is to provide age-appropriate alternatives that are neutral, even if a bit icky.

Don't Be in a Hurry

You may have heard it takes 21 days to break a bad habit or create a new one.

Unfortunately, that's a myth based on a misunderstanding of a study from the 1960s on self-image, not on habits. More recent studies have shown it takes anywhere from 18 days to 254 days for people to form a new habit. The average is 66 days.[2]

If you're a parent trying to correct a negative habit, that's certainly not what you want to hear. Still, if you recognize it will take some time—maybe even two to eight months—then you'll be less frustrated by unrealistic expectations.

PART 7

SKILLS AND HABITS FOR ENGAGING CULTURE

How to Look at Art

By learning how to look at art, we can gain exposure to worldviews (both Christian and non-Christian) and possibly even valuable insights into them. In developing the skill, we begin to discern the underlying worldview of the artist and equip ourselves to see what Nicholas Wolterstorff calls the world behind a work of art, "that complex of the artist's beliefs and goals, convictions and concerns, which play a role in accounting for the existence and character of the work."[1] Similarly, Francis Schaeffer says that "art forms add strength to the world view which shows through, no matter what the world view is or whether the world view is true or false."[2] Calvin Seerveld writes,

> Art is a symbolically significant expression of what drives a human heart, with what vision the artist views the world, how the artist adores whom. Art tells tales in whose service the artist stands because art itself is always a consecrated offering, a disconcertingly undogmatic yet terribly moving attempt to bring honor and glory and power to something.[3]

Knowing how to examine artwork can be valuable for shaping our own worldview and understanding the worldview of others. But the importance of art—and this is an essential point of clarification—is not found in any instrumental value, including its usefulness for worldview analysis.

The first and most important point a Christian should know about art, says Schaeffer, is that a work of art has value in itself. H.R. Rookmaaker agrees:

Art needs no justification. The mistake of many art theorists (and not only of Christian ones) is to try to give art a meaning or a sense by showing that it "does something." So art must open people's eyes, or serve as decoration, or prophesy, or praise, or have a social function, or express a particular philosophy. Art needs no such excuse. It has its own meaning that does not need to be explained, just as marriage does, or man himself, or the existence of a particular bird or flower or mountain or sea or star. These all have meaning because God has made them. Their meaning is that they have been created by God and are sustained by Him. So art has a meaning as art because God thought it good to give art and beauty to humanity.[4]

We are free to look at works of art for pleasure. We don't always need to search for their meaning or to uncover the worldview of the artist. Simply because we have a tool does not mean we must always use it.

Nevertheless, to look at art and see a worldview is a valuable skill to develop. Let's consider how we can look at art in this way.

Visual Arts

The arts that primarily engage our sight—as opposed to hearing, taste, smell, or touch—are the visual arts, such as painting, sculpture, photography, and architecture. These visual arts aren't necessarily higher forms than others, such as culinary or musical arts, but they are the ones in which worldviews tend to be perceived more clearly.

See the Art, Not the Artist

In looking at art for the purposes of worldview, we are attempting to identify the worldview content of the art itself, not necessarily the worldview of the artist. The worldview of the artist may not match the worldview they display through their art. As Schaeffer notes, the realm of art includes four kinds of people:

The first is the born-again man who writes or paints within the Christian total world view. The second is the non-Christian who expresses his own non-Christian world view. The third is the man who is personally a non-Christian but nevertheless writes or paints on the basis of the Christian consensus by which he has been influenced. The fourth person is the born-again Christian who does not understand what the total Christian world view should be and therefore produces art which embodies a non-Christian world view.[5]

This dissonance explains why looking at the artist's larger body of work, rather than a single item, is necessary when determining the worldview content.

The Look-See-Think Approach

Art historian Kit Messham-Muir outlines a simple three-step method we can use for analyzing a work of art.[6]

Look. The first step is to take the time to look at the work. Studies and surveys taken in art museums show most people don't spend much time looking at artwork. The Louvre found that people looked at the *Mona Lisa,* one of the world's most famous paintings, for an average of only 15 seconds.[7] We can't begin to understand a work of visual art until we've spent sufficient time simply looking to see what it entails.

See. What's the difference between looking and seeing in the context of art? "Looking is about literally describing what is in front of you, while seeing is about applying meaning to it," says Messham-Muir. At this stage we can ask four simple questions:

- What can I see just by looking at this artwork?
- How was this artwork made?
- When was it made, and what was happening in art and history at that time?
- Why did the artist create this work, and what is its meaning to them and to us now?[8]

Think. "The final step involves thinking about what you've observed," says Messham-Muir, "drawing together what you've gleaned from the first two steps and thinking about possible meanings." At this step we make a judgment about the work. Schaeffer recommends applying these basic standards:

- *Technical excellence.* Does the work exhibit a high degree of skill or talent? "If the artist's technical excellence is high, he is to be praised for this, even if we differ with his world view," says Schaeffer. "Man must be treated fairly as man."

- *Validity*. As Schaeffer explains, validity means "whether an artist is honest to himself and to his world view or whether he makes his art only for money or for the sake of being accepted."

- *Content (the worldview)*. "As far as a Christian is concerned, the world view that is shown through a body of art must be seen ultimately in terms of the Scripture," says Schaeffer. "The artist's world view is not to be free from the judgment of the Word of God."

Tips for Training Children

Enjoy Before Examining

A significant danger in teaching worldview analysis of art is that it can override the pleasures of experiencing great works of art. Expose them early and don't begin to teach them to be critical until after they gain a deep understanding that works of art can be valuable simply because they exhibit the creativity given to us by our Creator.

Push Against the Grain

The look-see-think approach requires sustained effort and attention, so children will be more likely to apply it to works of art that readily spark their imagination and capture their interest. Later, when they've developed the habit, you can encourage them to apply their critical skills to a broader range of works.

The Freedom to Be Wrong

Ask the child open-ended questions about artwork and then give them broad freedom in how they answer and interpret. Although a subjective element exists in all interpretation of art, the child may entirely miss the point the artist was intending to make. Emphasize what they might not have observed, but avoid shutting down their perspective, lest they think art is like mathematics and they are expected to discover the one right answer.

Capture More Information

After learning to apply the look-see-think approach, give them additional tools to see even more. The theologian and visual artist Fred Sanders offers several helpful suggestions for how to gain more from a viewing.[9]

Define the moment. Most every artwork captures a moment in time. Sanders recommends asking, why does this image capture precisely the moment it does? If it were a photo, could it have been taken one second earlier? Ten seconds? Is there a decisive instant in time which the image captures? What is that instant?

Reconstruct it in your mind. Mentally disassemble the art object you're looking at and ask yourself how it was put together in the first place, says Sanders. By thinking about how the work was constructed—how the paint was applied or the marble was carved—we can gain a better understanding of why the artist made the choices they did.

Let the artist guide your eyes. "You may notice that parts of the painting are hard to focus on, while other parts keep drawing your eyes in with a kind of visual magnetism," says Sanders.

> The artist has worked hard to draw your attention where he wants it, and to keep your attention from being able to linger in other places. Some sections seem brightly lit and sharply focused, while others are dark, hazy, and blurred. You may find your eyes making a circular swooping motion, or sliding off the left side of the image and having to jump back in to the middle. All of that is by design, and as you warm up to a piece, you should entrust your eyes to the visual and compositional forces which the artist has marshalled for that reason. The better the artist is, the more you can trust him to do the right thing with your eyes.

Use background knowledge. The more you know about the artist and their work, the more you can apply that knowledge to analyses of individual pieces. "If you know something about the artist in question or the image you're looking at, go ahead and bring that information to bear on it," says Sanders. "It's fine to say, 'Michelangelo was a Platonist' as you study his work, and see if you can find connections between what you're seeing in front of you and what you already knew."

How to Listen to Music

Should parents be concerned about the music their children listen to? The answer used to be rather obvious. The influence of music, especially on the young, was a primary concern for thousands of years. The ancient Greek philosopher Plato was so wary of the power of music, he believed it should be controlled by the state. And the eighteenth-century Scottish politician Andrew Fletcher boldly claimed, "If one were permitted to make all the ballads, one need not care who should make the laws of a nation."

But a shift started around the 1950s as pop music began to target young people rather than older adults. Concern about what kids were listening to peaked in the late 1980s when Tipper Gore and the Parents Music Resource Center lobbied the music industry to have parental advisory stickers put on albums that had music containing violent, drug-related, or sexual themes. (The labels are still there, but now that music is downloadable, the warnings aren't as effective.)

Most parents today grew up with those labels on our music. And many of us listened to music in our youth that would have shocked our parents and that we'd never let our children listen to today. This may leave us conflicted and feeling a bit hypocritical about trying to control what music we allow our own kids to enjoy. Ultimately, every parent must decide where they draw the line on pop music. But we should not fool ourselves into thinking the decision is inconsequential. To paraphrase Andrew Fletcher, if one were permitted to make all the songs, one need not care who should make the theology of a nation. For better or for worse, your child's worldview will be shaped by the music they listen to.

How then should we address the role of music in our child's life? By focusing on a simple, broad principle: focus on the lyrics.

This is not to say musical styles or genres cannot affect us or our children. They may certainly affect our emotions, and we might want to avoid certain types based on our temperament. (For example, someone with an anxious disposition may find heavy metal music to be nerve-racking.) However, we should not confuse our individual distaste for a style with a biblical prohibition against all forms of that music. You may not appreciate country or rap, but God hasn't issued a ban on those styles.

When it comes to music, the concern comes not from the chords on the guitar or the beats on the drum but from the lyrics that flow from the tongue. As Jesus says, "The words you speak come from the heart—that's what defiles you" (Matthew 15:18 NLT). The lyrics can make a song "worldly" in the sense of dishonoring Christ by being conformed to the attitudes and values of an unredeemed culture.

Does this mean we should avoid all music not produced by Christians? No. God made the world, and though it is fallen, his grace still shines through. For example, God created the institution of marriage between a man and a woman—and not just between Christian men and Christian women. We can therefore enjoy songs that praise the good of marriage or the love between a married couple. Similarly, we can enjoy music that recognizes or acknowledges the sinfulness of the world in a way that does not glorify or condone it.

At least we can as adults. Children may not be able to make those distinctions, which is why they need to be trained to listen not only with their ears but with their heart. By teaching them how to listen to and evaluate the content of lyrics, we can help them listen with discernment.

Tips for Training Children

Control What Comes into Your Home

As a parent, you wouldn't allow your kids to read *Playboy* or watch an X-rated movie. Similarly, we shouldn't turn a blind eye or a deaf ear to the descriptions of pornographic acts set to the beat of a drum machine found in much pop music. We can't control the music throughout the state, as Plato wished, or even control all the music our child hears when they are out of the house. But we have the power and authority to control what comes into our homes.

Do Your Homework

When it comes to educating yourself about pop music, you have an advantage your parents likely didn't have: the internet. Today, doing your homework on the content of music is easier and cheaper than in previous generations. You can hear a sample of almost any song your child wants to listen to and read the lyrics for free. Spend the time researching the artists and songs that capture their imagination so you can have an informed discussion about their musical preferences.

Don't Settle for Shallow Justifications

Your child wants to fit in with the rest of culture, so be ready to hear every excuse imaginable for why they should listen to "worldly" music:

"I just like the beat. I'm not even paying attention to the lyrics."

"But the singer is a Christian. They even thanked God at the Grammys."

"Sure, it contains bad language, but I hear worse from the kids at school."

Don't concede to such shallow justifications. They may be plausible; they may even be true. But giving in to them won't help your child become a more God-honoring believer.

Focus on Their Present Condition, Not Their Future Rebellion

When it comes to parenting, the most misused Bible verse is likely Proverbs 22:6: "Start children off on the way they should go, and even when they are old they will not turn from it." Too many parents treat this verse as if it's a promise attached to a command rather than what it is—a proverb (a general truth).

But the verse is a proverb because it *is* generally true. If we start children off on the way they should go by limiting their exposure to unedifying music, they are indeed more likely to avoid such music when they are older. Too often, though, we focus too much on the future—specifically, the child's potential rebellion. We worry that if we're too strict now regarding what they listen to, then they'll rebel when they get older. Perhaps they will. But so what? Why should we allow their worldview to be corrupted now—at an age when they are most impressionable—simply to avoid their listening to the same type of music when they are older?

As parents, we can control the input but not the outcome. Do your part by showing them the way they should go today and trust God to lead them in the future.

Listen to Music Together

This can be the hardest advice to follow, especially if you do not share your teen's musical taste. But listening to music together can help clarify for your child why certain songs are problematic. Remind them that if they are ashamed to listen to racy or violent music in your presence, they should be even more concerned about listening to it in the presence of our holy God.

How to Watch a Movie

Having considered how to look at art and how to listen to music, why do we need to think about how to watch a movie? Many of the same principles in chapters 35 and 36 apply to movies, but considering movies in a separate category is helpful for two reasons.

First, movies tend to present a broader range of themes and perspectives than mainstream pop music or modern art. They are thus more effective at conveying worldviews and worthy of special scrutiny.

Second, of the dominant pop culture art forms, film and TV have the largest shared audience. You can't expect your friends and coworkers to have read a certain newly released novel. Aside from a select few bestselling works of mystery or horror, almost no works of new fiction are being read by even your book-loving acquaintances. As for music, technology has led to increasing fragmentation. A few ubiquitous chart-topping hits may be known to the majority, but most people's musical taste is cordoned off into narrow genres or even sub-genres. That leaves movies and television as the last remaining cultural media widely shared across demographic lines.

Knowing how to watch movies—not only to enjoy them but also to consider them as works of art and conveyors of worldviews—is thus a skill that helps us better understand our culture and engage with our neighbors.

Increasing your knowledge about an art form will increase your artistic appreciation and hone your critical insight. But to become a more discerning critic of film (and to teach your child to be one too), you don't need a degree in film studies. You don't even need to know what a grip does or what *mise-en-scène* means. You only need to learn a few new concepts, apply a few techniques, and ask a few thought-provoking questions. Here are some recommendations to get you started on the path to becoming a discerning film critic.

The Basics of Film Grammar

Grammar is the structural system that governs how we use language. You can understand this sentence because you learned the rules of English grammar. Film also has its own grammar.

- A *frame* is a single still image. It is analogous to a letter.
- A *shot* is a single continuous recording made by a camera. It is analogous to a word.
- A *scene* is a series of related shots. It is analogous to a sentence. A transition between scenes—dissolve, fade to black, direct cut, and so on—is called "film punctuation."
- A *sequence* is a series of scenes that tell a major part of an entire story. It is analogous to a paragraph.[1]

A Simple Method for Studying a Film

The late Roger Ebert was an influential film critic and a renowned teacher of film criticism. He had a simple yet profound method of studying film he believed anyone could apply: "Just pause the film and think about what you see."[2]

The ground rules he used in class, Ebert said, are that "Anybody could call out 'stop!' and discuss what we were looking at, or whatever had just occurred to them." (This approach won't work, of course, when you're seeing the film in the theater. But it can be used at home or anywhere else where you watch a movie that can be paused.)

Pay Attention

If the movie is worth your time, it is worth your attention. You don't necessarily need to apply your full attention and critical skills to every movie, but in general the more you actively engage with the film, the more you'll understand. If you take the time to study a movie using the approach listed above, you should focus on a few key elements. Here are some ideas of what to pay attention to and a sample question to consider for each.[3]

- Plot: What was the movie about?
- Themes and tone: What was the central goal of the movie?
- Acting and characters: Did the acting support the characters and help them come to life?
- Direction: How did the director's choices affect the storytelling?
- Score: Did the music support the mood of the movie?
- Cinematography: Were the shots used in a unique way to tell the story?
- Production design: Did the created environments heighten the atmosphere on camera?
- Special effects: Were the special effects integrated well to the purpose of the story?
- Editing: Was the flow of the film consistent?
- Pace: Did the movie flow well?
- Dialogue: Did the words match the tone of the movie and personality of the characters?

As you begin paying attention to these 11 elements, you'll soon notice you have certain specific concerns or interests. Use what captures your attention to form questions that will help you evaluate movies.

Roger's Rules of Thumb

To understand what is going on in a frame, shot, scene, or sequence, we need to focus on the 11 elements listed above. But movies are told from a unique perspective defined by the director's placement of the camera. We therefore also need to aware of the choices the director is making and what they might mean. Ebert had a few rules of thumb that can help us understand the meaning of what is being shown in the frame or shot.

> Right is more positive, left more negative. Movement to the right seems more favorable; to the left, less so. The future seems to live on the right,

the past on the left. The top is dominant over the bottom. The foreground is stronger than the background. Symmetrical compositions seem at rest. Diagonals in a composition seem to 'move' in the direction of the sharpest angle they form, even though of course they may not move at all. Therefore, a composition could lead us into a background that becomes dominant over a foreground. Tilt shots of course put everything on a diagonal, implying the world is out of balance. I have the impression that more tilts are down to the right than to the left, perhaps suggesting the characters are sliding perilously into their futures. Left tilts to me suggest helplessness, sadness, resignation. Few tilts feel positive. Movement is dominant over things that are still. A POV above a character's eyeline reduces him; below the eyeline, enhances him. Extreme high angle shots make characters into pawns; low angles make them into gods. Brighter areas tend to be dominant over darker areas, but far from always: Within the context, you can seek the "dominant contrast," which is the area we are drawn toward. Sometimes it will be darker, further back, lower, and so on. It can be as effective to go against intrinsic weightings as to follow them.[4]

If you're interested in learning other rules of thumb about shot composition, numerous online videos are available that break down shots and scenes from famous movies and explain why the directors made the choices they did and how it affected the stories they were telling.

Tips for Training Children

Ask Questions

If a child is old enough to watch a movie, they are old enough to do so with discernment—which means they are old enough to become a film critic. We can't expect an elementary-age child to be a sophisticated movie reviewer, but by asking probing questions, we can develop them into more insightful consumers of film culture. For example, don't just ask, "Did you like the movie?" but instead ask focused questions, such as, "What did you like about the main character?"

As the child matures, you can incorporate questions that go deeper in exploring the worldview presented in the film. William D. Romanowski offers several examples of questions to consider:[5]

- What ideals, values, beliefs, attitudes, and assumptions are being displayed? Which ones are glamorized or denigrated?

- From whose perspective is the story told?

- What motivates the characters?

- Does the film present a moral universe? From the perspective of the film, what constitutes good and bad conduct?

- Does God exist in the film, or are the events and affairs directed by human effort alone?

- What authority exists other than self?

These are but examples of the types of questions your child should consider when watching movies. Create your own list and use it to study a film together with your child.

Moral Versus Christian

Moral lessons may be commendable without being distinctly Christian, since Hindus, Muslims, and ethical humanists could agree with them. And mere optimistic positive messages are not enough and may even be harmful, since they can create the illusion we can achieve righteousness by our own efforts. This can be true even for movies marketed as being Christian films.

What then does it take for a film to be Christian, whether indirectly or explicitly? As Gene Veith explains, "All distinctly Christian art must be, in some sense, about the agonizing struggle between sin and grace."[6] To be Christian, a work needs to include themes of sin and grace and what Christ has to do with them.

We don't necessarily need to limit our viewing habits to films that are, by this definition, Christian, but we should refrain from giving the label "Christian" to works that don't fit this definition. Teach your child to recognize the difference so they don't confuse a Christian worldview with one that promotes a secular form of righteousness.

Look for More Than Sanctified Tropes

Over the past few decades, a popular approach to Christian film criticism is to search for redemptive themes. This usually entails identifying an element necessary for distinctly Christian art—such as the agonizing struggle between sin and grace—and using it as a justification to sanctify the movie. Too often, the supposedly redemptive theme is nothing more than the use of a trope (a common or overused theme), such as death and resurrection (the hero comes close to death but rises to fight on) or the "Christ figure" (where a character is similar to Jesus in a usually indirect manner).

Any moderately competent director can turn Satan into a "Christ figure," but that wouldn't give the movie a redemptive theme. By using this technique, though, many Christians justify watching just about anything, including films that include pornography and senseless violence. We need to teach children to distinguish between actual redemptive themes and mere tropes so they don't fool themselves into watching material they know is harmful to their souls.

38

How to Consume the News

What exactly is the news? Who decides what constitutes news? What makes news important? What is the purpose of the news for the individual? What distinguishes news from mere gossip, ephemera, or trivia? How should Christians relate to news? Although these questions have significant worldview implications, they are rarely considered, and few parents help their children think about these issues.

Let's start with the easiest one, the definition. For our purposes, we'll use the term "news" the way it's used most commonly in our daily lives—information about current events delivered to the public by the news media. Regarding the second question—who decides what constitutes news—since the news is the product of the news media, those media determines what constitutes news. The news is a product to be consumed in a brief time—daily, if not hourly—so we'll come back for more.

The question of what makes news important is more difficult. The *New York Times* publishes 150 articles a day Monday through Saturday, and 250 articles on Sunday.[1] On a planet of 7.6 billion people, there must be more than 150 important events occurring every day. Yet news outlets like the *New York Times* determine what is important enough (or what will sell enough papers) to constitute the day's news.

What is the purpose of the news to individuals? The answer to this one is likely not what you'd think. Most people would say the purpose of the news is to keep the average person informed. But few people even know about, much less read, the 1,150 news items produced by the *New York Times* each week. And those are just the current events a single media outlet considers newsworthy.

What distinguishes news from mere gossip, ephemera, or trivia? The answer should include an explanation of how the story fits into a broader narrative or has an air of permanence. But news, especially daily news, is often presented in a way that strips it of its context. C. John Sommerville explains this in an article titled "Why the News Makes Us Dumb":

> What happens when you sell information on a daily basis? You have to make each day's report seem important, and you do this primarily by reducing the importance of its context. What you are selling is change, and if readers were aware of the bigger story, that would tend to diminish today's contribution. The industry has to convince its consumers of the significance of today's News, and it has to make them want to come back tomorrow for more News—more change. The implication will then be that today's report can now be forgotten. So News involves a radical devaluation of the past, and short-circuits any kind of debate.[2]

In his book of the same title, Sommerville makes this even clearer:

> The product of the news business is change, not wisdom. Wisdom has to do with seeing things in their largest context, whereas news is structured in a way that destroys the larger context. You have to do certain things to information if you want to sell it on a daily basis. You have to make each day's report seem important. And you do that by reducing the importance of its context.[3]

This focus on change, devoid of context and connection to a greater reality, makes daily news an impediment to the acquisition of two things Christians should be seeking: wisdom and understanding (Proverbs 4:5). As Sommerville says, the news industry must do certain things to information to sell it to us every day. We therefore also must do certain things to information to ensure the news doesn't make us "dumber" and to use it in a way that helps us gain wisdom and understanding. Here are a few ways Christians can relate to the news.

Consider What You Believe About the News

Which is more important to us, God's Word or the news? What if someone were asked to determine that answer by observing our habits? What would they conclude?

The uncomfortable truth is we often spend far more time reading newspapers than reading the Bible. And we spend more time watching news programs than actively acquiring wisdom. How would your life differ if you changed your news consumption habits to reflect what you wanted to believe about the value of news in developing wisdom and understanding?

Consume Less News Product

Most news product is the mental and spiritual equivalent of junk food. By consuming less of it, we won't necessarily improve our health, but we can limit its negative effects on us. But what if we miss something? Media theorist Neil Postman offers this response:

> If you are concerned that cutting down your viewing time will cause you to "miss" important news, keep this in mind: each day's TV news consists for the most part, of fifteen examples of the Seven Deadly Sins, with which you are already quite familiar. There may be a couple of stories exemplifying lust, usually four about murder, occasionally one about gluttony, another about envy, and so on. It cannot possibly do you any harm to excuse yourself each week from thirty or forty of these examples. Remember: TV news does not reflect normal, everyday life.[4]

While this advice is helpful for adults, it is doubly so for children and teens.

Seek Out Actionable News

Much of the news we consume either has no direct effect on our lives or is information we will not act on. We should know some news items because they affect our neighbors, but we should focus on news that is actionable, that we can directly affect. This is why local news is often more important, since there is a greater likelihood it will be something we can directly engage with. At a minimum, we can act by praying about the people and events we encounter in the news.

Ask the Eternal Question

A fully developed Christian worldview will lead us to have an eternal perspective, viewing events not only in their historical but also their eschatological context (that which will last after the old creation passes away). Not much news will be of long-term consequence, yet we should frequently seek out news that will matter for all eternity. This means we can ignore much of the daily news since truly important events are rarely captured on the front page of a daily paper. Former news reporter Malcolm Muggeridge admits as much:

> I've often thought…that if I'd been a journalist in the Holy Land at the time of our Lord's ministry, I should have spent my time looking into what was happening in Herod's court. I'd be wanting to sign Salome for her exclusive memoirs, and finding out what Pilate was up to, and…I would have missed completely the most important event there ever was.[5]

Tips for Training Children

"Current Events" Curricula

There is no reason for children who are not yet high school age to regularly engage with daily news. Yet many schools, under the guise of helping children become informed, waste valuable class time on so-called current events. If possible, try to limit your child's news exposure at school. But if the teacher insists on including current events in the curricula, ask that it be provided in a broader context, such as connecting current controversies to historical trends.

Print, Radio, and TV News

Teens will eventually develop habits when consuming news product. We can positively shape their consumption by teaching them to get the bulk of their news in printed form (including online text), to listen to radio news sparingly, and to avoid TV news like it's spreading a plague (which it is, if we consider stupidity to be contagious).

The primary reason for developing this preference is the way each medium communicates information. Television has a lower informational density than a newspaper. All the words spoken in an hour of TV news could fit on a single page of a newspaper, says Postman, so TV viewers are getting much less news content than newspaper readers.[6] Postman also notes, "The grammar of images is weak in communicating past-ness and present-ness" and prefers change rather than stasis. That's why, says Postman, violence finds its way on television news so often—it is a radical and attention-grabbing form of change.

Old News for News Skills

Most of what occurs daily is inconsequential and not worth your child's time. Sommerville proposes a test:

> Still dubious about all this? Consider the proposition: If it is no longer worth your while to go back and read the News of, oh, September 22, 1976, then it was never worthwhile doing so. And why should today be any different?[7]

Most of us wouldn't think it was worth our time to read a newspaper from yesterday, much less one from 1976. But "old news" can be a useful tool for teaching teenagers how to engage with news product.

Find a newsmagazine published 30 to 60 days ago and a current daily newspaper (print versions work best for this exercise). Have the child compare and contrast both publications so they can answer these questions:

- What news items appear in both? What does that tell us about their significance?

- What items were considered important in the newsmagazine but were not deemed worthy of continued coverage in the newspaper?

- What predictions were made in the newsmagazine? Did they come to pass? What predictions are being made in the current paper?

By asking questions such as these, you can help your teen distinguish between trivia and trends. Having them carry out this project on a regular interval (such as once a month) and comparing what they learn each time can help them develop the skill of engaging critically with the news.

News Specialists

The most useful way to consume news product effectively is to specialize. Rather than having teens become shallowly informed about all current events, encourage them to choose one to three topics of interest to follow in the news.

(These areas of interest should be ones they'll also read books about.) By keeping up with the same subjects they'll be better equipped to identify significant long-term trends and to put new information into a broader context. This will lead to a narrower specialization, of course, but they'll be better prepared to use the news to gain wisdom and understanding.

PART 8

SKILLS AND HABITS FOR LEARNING

How to Study

Developing a fully functional Christian worldview requires a vast amount of knowledge about God and his creation. As Francis Bacon wrote, "There are two books laid before us to study, to prevent our falling into error; first, the volume of Scriptures, which reveal the will of God; then the volume of the Creatures, which express His power."[1] To be a Christian means to be a lifelong student, which entails a lifetime of study.

Study is the application of the mind to the acquisition of knowledge, as by reading, investigation, or reflection.[2] While the term "study" is often treated as a synonym for "learn," the concepts are distinct. We can learn without studying and study without learning. Studying is a means of learning. The goal is not to study for the sake of studying. The goal of study is to learn.

For our purposes, we'll narrow it down even further and consider the purpose of all studying, as Jim Roth says, to be to "keep The Curve of Forgetting from affecting your recall and ability to use what you have learned."[3]

The Curve of Forgetting

The Curve of Forgetting (originally called the Ebbinghaus Curve, after the German philosopher Hermann Ebbinghaus, who developed it in 1885) describes how new information we learn is lost over time when we don't make regular effort to retain it.

Imagine, for example, your child learns new information in a lecture at school. At that point, they retain nearly 100 percent of the information. After

24 hours, if no additional effort is made, the child will only retain about 60 percent of the information. After 48 hours, it will decline to about 40 percent. Within 30 days, the child will retain only 2 or 3 percent of the information they had "learned."

Fortunately, there's a simple and easy way to reshift the curve and retain the information, as the University of Waterloo explains:

> Here's the formula and the case for making time to review material: within 24 hours of getting the information—spend 10 minutes reviewing and you will raise the curve almost to 100% again. A week later (day 7), it only takes 5 minutes to "reactivate" the same material, and again raise the curve. By day 30, your brain will only need 2-4 minutes to give you the feedback, "yes, I know that."[4]

As the article notes, "Often students feel they can't possibly make time for a review session every day in their schedules—they have trouble keeping up as it is." This is why the time set aside for homework is essential (see below). By having a dedicated time set aside every day for a mini review of previously learned information, the process will become an ingrained habit. Not only will this approach save them time and energy they'd waste cramming for a test (an ineffective approach), they'll feel less stressed and anxious about tests since they are better able to remember the material they learned.

The Question and Answer Format

What is the best method for remembering and retaining the information? Roth suggests the question and answer format:

> Always study in Question/Answer format. In other words, whether you are reading a textbook chapter or going over your lecture notes, you should always be looking for an answer to a question you have created to focus your attention. In addition, the question/answer format is precisely the format of a test. Studying in this format means that you immediately begin learning the information in the way a test will ask it. Remember—it is possible to learn the right information in the wrong way and fail a test.[5]

Now that you know the purpose of studying is to increase the recall of what you've learned and the best approach for this purpose is the question and answer format, you can understand why flash cards are such powerful study tools. Using the Leitner system, you can supercharge the process of studying. Here's how it works.

1. Get a stack of index cards, a box to hold the cards, and three dividers (you can label them 1, 2, and 3).

2. Write your question on the front of the card and the answer on the back. Include only one term, question, idea, or list on a card.

3. Put all the cards with your questions and answers in the middle section, behind divider 2.

4. Review your cards. If you get the answer right, put the card into section 1. If you get it wrong, put it in 3.

5. Review each card every day until the cards are sorted into two categories—1 and 3.

6. Review the cards in 3 every day and the ones in 1 every other day or every third day.

7. Repeat until all the cards are in 1 and then review at regular intervals (30 days, 60 days, and so on).

If you produce a relevant set of questions and answers and review the material regularly, you'll be amazed at how much you'll have improved your ability to recall what you've learned.

Tips for Training Children

Unlearning Bad Habits

Many parents don't give serious attention to their child's study habits until sometime between middle school and high school. By the time we recognize their need to develop effective study habits, they've already spent years creating ineffective approaches. If you find yourself in this situation, don't despair—bad habits can be unlearned. But if possible, start thinking about how you'll teach your child to study before they start their first day of kindergarten.

Homework Every Day

Never ask your child if they have homework—they do. Even if their teacher has not sent home extra work to do, the child will need to overcome the curve of forgetting. They need a time set aside in their schedule—preferably a regular time, four to six days a week—to apply the methods for reviewing the material they've learned. At a minimum, they'll need 20 to 30 minutes—in addition to any homework assigned by the teacher.

Metacognition

Experiments have shown one of the most effective strategies for improving studying and learning is metacognition—thinking about thinking. This means you'll need to develop a plan that helps your child think about how they think, and develop a strategy for how they'll study. All it takes is to come up with some relevant questions to spur their thinking about how to approach their study and what the end goal is they hope to achieve.

Here are some metacognitive, goal-oriented prompts.

- "What grade do you want to get on the upcoming test?" Encourage them to be as specific as possible, such as "at least a 92" or "B-plus."

- "On a scale of 1 to 5, with 5 being the most important, how important is getting that grade?"

- "On a scale of 1 to 5, with 5 being the most likely, how likely are you to get that grade?"

Be wary of setting the goals and expectations too high, and be realistic about your child's capabilities. This strategy has been shown to be effective in improving a student's performance by an average of one-third of a letter grade.[6] Push for improvement, not perfection. If you expect every child to say that it's important to get an A-plus and that it's highly likely they'll do so, you'll merely teach them to tell you what they think you want to hear.

Next, prompt them to consider study strategies to achieve the goal they set for themselves. Have them consider what study resources are available (such as flash cards, class notes, and peer tutoring) and then rank which are most likely to help them learn the material.

Asking these questions may seem like procrastination from studying, but research has shown they are among the top most effective strategies for improving learning performance.

40

How to Become a Better Learner

ntelligent people are always ready to learn," says Proverbs. "Their ears are open for knowledge" (18:15 NLT). Because we need extensive knowledge to become fully formed followers of Jesus, a willingness to learn is a core aspect of the Christian life. But even when we want to learn, when our "ears are open for knowledge," we may struggle because we've never developed the habits that can make our learning effective.

These recommendations for improving your ability to acquire new knowledge and skills are based on the work of Ulrich Boser, author of the book *Learn Better.*[1]

Find the Value

If you took algebra in school, you probably asked, "When are we ever going to use this?" And if you asked that question, you probably don't remember much from that class. To effectively learn a subject or skill, we must be motivated to learn and have a meaningful connection to what we are learning. When learning a new subject, search for why it's valuable to you. Will it help you do your job more effectively? Will it improve your relationships? Will it give you a greater understanding of God?

Knowledge Built on Knowledge

To gain new knowledge we must build on the knowledge we already possess. There is no learning without prior knowledge, says Boser. "We understand things through the prism of what we know," he adds, "and anything that we want to learn is based on what we've already learned." This means we'll need to identify the background knowledge our child currently possesses and connect it to the new material to be learned.

Mixed Practice

One of the most enduring conclusions from the new science of learning is the idea that people gain more if they mix up their practice. Researcher after researcher argues that people shouldn't repeat a skill during a learning or training session…

Whether we're learning how to knit or deep sea dive, a mixed up approach helps us see past the surface details and gain a richer understanding, and when people see multiple examples with different details, they're far more likely to develop important insights into a skill or area of knowledge.

Psychologists sometimes call the practice "interleaving" or "jumbling," and a wealth of research provides support for the approach. In one study from the 1990s, some young women learned to fire off foul shots. Some practiced only foul shots. Others took more of a mixed up approach—they practiced foul shots as well as eight and fifteen footers.

The results were remarkable: The mixed-shot group performed much better, with a much deeper sense of the underlying skill. The same is true in academic fields, from memory tests to problem solving skills: By mixing up practice, people develop a better sense of the underlying ideas, and they'll sometimes post outcomes as much as 40% higher than those using a blocked approach.[2]

Create a Feedback Loop

"In order to develop any sort of skill, you need to know what you know—and what you need to change," says Boser. To know what we need to change often requires that we get some sort of external feedback. Having someone examine our progress and tell us what we are getting wrong can help us rapidly correct and improve our learning process.

Tips for Training Children

Tell the Truth About Learning

Learning is hard work. Kids not only need to know this, they need to know *we* know this. If we give a child the impression all learning should be fun and easy, they'll be discouraged when they discover it can be dull and difficult. Teach them that when it comes to learning, what matters is not how smart they are but how gritty they are, and that perseverance is more important than natural brainpower.

Finding the Value—and Being Patient

Whenever possible, give your child a modicum of control over how they will learn. Identify the outcome you want them to gain from the learning and then give them the freedom to choose a path to that goal. Be prepared, though, for this approach to take longer. Most learning in school is designed to be applied to a mass audience (as with standardized curriculum and tests) so it can be done quickly and efficiently. Projects that allow for independence may take longer, but by gaining a meaningful connection, your child will learn the material at a deeper level.

Determine What They Know

If your child is struggling to learn something new, review their base of knowledge. Start by considering what knowledge they need before learning the new material. If they're having trouble learning how to use fractions, for instance, they may need to review what they know about division. Remind them that what they are learning is an extension of what they already know. Don't take for granted they can make such connections themselves.

Let Them Struggle

Since learning is hard, children need to be taught to struggle and persevere. It's all too easy for us to get frustrated and bored when teaching our children and to just give them the answer. By letting them do the hard work of learning, we are making the information more meaningful and helping them learn the invaluable skill of learning.

Provide Positive Feedback

Having people tell us what we are getting wrong is almost always painful or humiliating. Even when we know we need to improve, having someone point it out can be tough to hear. This is especially true for children who tend to seek validation from their parents.

Provide a positive feedback loop by pointing out what they are doing right before showing them what they are doing wrong. Don't get upset when they grow frustrated. Instead, assure them that with time and effort they'll be able to learn the new skill.

41

How to Memorize Almost Anything

In the medieval era, almost all Christian clergy and educated laity were expected to have memorized significant portions of the Bible. Even before being accepted as a monk, a man was expected to have memorized all 150 psalms. For church fathers like Augustine, memorization of the biblical text helped to make Scripture function like a second language. It has been observed, says Mary Carruthers, that Augustine wrote "not only in Latin but 'in Psalms,' so imbued is his language with their phrasing and vocabulary."[1]

When we speak of "devouring a book," we are following the lead of our medieval ancestors, who considered the stomach a metaphor for memory. Books like the Bible were devoured, digested, and regurgitated for recitation. As the Italian poet Petrarch said, "I ate in the morning what I would digest in the evening; I swallowed as a boy what I would ruminate upon as an older man."

How many of us can say we've swallowed Scripture in a way that allows us to ruminate on God's Word?

But the craft of memorization is not just for our internal use. Like most crafts, it has practical application. "As an art, memory was most importantly associated in the Middles Ages with composition, not simply with retention," says Carruthers. "Those who practiced the crafts of memory used them—as all crafts are used—to make new things: prayers, meditations, sermons, pictures, hymns, stories, and poems."

Memorization is an essential aspect of the stewardship of our imagination, but it has been all but lost. You can recover this forgotten skill and pass it along to your children with some simple techniques.

You don't have to have a good memory (whatever that means) to fill your imagination with Scripture and knowledge about the Bible. By the time you finish this chapter, you'll have learned how to memorize lists (such as the Ten Commandments).

In this chapter you'll learn four tips that will show you how to apply this process to remembering lists of items and how to store them in a "memory palace" so you can instantly recall an extraordinary amount of information.

After reading this chapter, you can turn back to chapter 13, "How to Memorize the Biblical Narrative," and learn how to apply these skills to remember every key event in Genesis (the first step in memorizing the entire narrative structure of the Bible, including details about hundreds of persons and events).

A Ridiculous Method

The art of memory, as Ed Cooke explains in his book *Remember, Remember,* is the "art of making sure what you give your mind to remember is as bright and amusing and energetic and outrageous as possible."[2] You are unlikely to forget information when it has been associated with a vivid image.

To quickly and easily remember any new piece of information, associate it with something you already know or remember *in some ridiculous way.* Those last four words are essential to effective memorization—and the reason why many people who have been taught memory techniques do not apply them. The technique seems silly because it *is* silly. For some reason, God designed our brains to remember things that are absurd and unusual. This fact didn't bother giants of the faith like Augustine and Thomas Aquinas, so it shouldn't bother you either. Fortunately, it likely won't bother children who use it, as early Christians did, to honor the Creator of our imaginations.

This is a skill that is easier to teach once you've learned to do it yourself. So let's put this concept into practice by memorizing these 20 items in sequence: otter, Thor, Zeus, American, idol, weather vane, ice cream sundae, parents, sleigh, adult, tree, steel, bear, false, eyelashes, watches, wife, ox, butler, and donkey.

You'll see associations between some of these words (such as Thor and Zeus, or otter, bear, ox, and donkey), but no obvious connection ties them together. You could use brute force (reciting the words over and over until you can repeat them verbatim), but that is too time consuming and not very effective. Instead, let's try to associate them in some ridiculous way.

Let's take the first five items—Otter, Thor, Zeus, American, idol—and combine them into a ridiculous but memorable mental picture. Since most people are familiar with the music competition show *American Idol*, let's combine those two words as the basis of our first vivid image.

Instead of the usual panel of judges on the television show, picture the guest judges as an *otter*, *Thor*, and *Zeus*. To make it easier to remember these items, give them an action: The *otter* loves the singers and is enthusiastically clapping. *Thor* too appreciates the music and is banging his hammer on the desk in approval. *Zeus*, however, is displeased and is throwing a lightning bolt at the contestants. (To remember them in order, be sure to see each one in turn, creating a vivid picture of them before moving on to the next.)

Now follow Zeus's lightning bolt as it misses the singers and hits the words *American Idol* in the logo behind the stage. The shocked duet that was singing are dressed as a *weather vane* and an *ice cream sundae*, but when you look closer you notice they are your own *parents* (or someone else's parents if that makes it easier to picture).

Frightened by the Greek god's action, the parents look for an escape. To their surprise (and ours), Santa Claus comes to the rescue, beckoning them to jump into his *sleigh*. As Santa rides off into the sky, the sleigh crashes into a very tall *adult tree* (the children trees on either side are unhurt). Santa and your parents fall out of the sleigh, but before they crash to the ground, they grab onto a *steel* beam that is sticking out of the side of a building.

The parents are barely hanging on by the tips of their fingers, but fortunately for them, underneath is a huge *bear* ready to catch them if they fall. The bear is rather peculiar looking, though—he is wearing large *false eyelashes* and two diamond-encrusted Rolex *watches*, one on each arm. Coming toward the hero are his bear *wife* riding an *ox* and his very human *butler* (dressed as a proper English servant), who is riding a *donkey*.

Now, before you do anything else, close your eyes and try to remember each of the items—starting with *otter*—by picturing them in the sequence of events.

Chances are you were not only able to remember at least 10 out of the 20 but were also able to remember their order. That's not bad for having merely read through the passage one time. If you spend an additional five to ten minutes reading through the list and sequence again and create clear mental images of each (particularly the ones you missed), you'll soon be able to recall all 20 perfectly.

The purpose of having you memorize this list of seemly random terms was mainly to show that you could, using absurd visual images, quickly and easily remember new information as well as the sequence in which it is presented. But you might have also noticed that the terms weren't chosen at random. Strung together they provide cues to remember the order of the Ten Commandments using terms that are the same or similar sounding.

1. "You shall have no other [*otter*] gods [*Thor, Zeus*] before me."

2. "You shall not make for yourself a carved image [idol—*American, idol*], or any likeness of anything that is in heaven above, or that is in the earth beneath, or that is in the water under the earth."

3. "You shall not take the name of the LORD your God in vain [*weather vane*], for the LORD will not hold him guiltless who takes his name in vain."

4. "Remember the Sabbath day [Sunday—*ice cream sundae*], to keep it holy."

5. "Honor your father and your mother [*parents*], that your days may be long in the land that the LORD your God is giving you."

6. "You shall not murder [slay—*sleigh*]."

7. "You shall not commit adultery [*adult, tree*]."

8. "You shall not steal [*steel*]."

9. "You shall not bear [*bear*] false [*false, eyelashes*] witness [*watches*] against your neighbor."

10. "You shall not covet your neighbor's house; you shall not covet your neighbor's wife [*wife*], or his male servant [*butler*], or his female

servant, or his ox [*ox*], or his donkey [*donkey*], or anything that is your neighbor's" (Exodus 20:3-17 esv).

If you are completely unfamiliar with the Ten Commandments, these cues are likely to be of no value. But if you have trouble remembering whether "You shall not steal" comes before or after "You shall not murder," they may help in learning the proper sequence.

Now that you know that you can memorize lists—and that it isn't as painful or difficult as you might have imagined—try memorizing another string of terms. Make a list of 10 to 20 words (preferably nouns), create an action-oriented image for each, and string them together in a simple story. Then test yourself to see how quickly you can memorize the words using your image-string-story technique.

Now that you've learned to create images and string them together to memorize lists, let's examine some of the ways you can expand on that technique to develop your ability to quickly and effectively memorize large collections of information.

Mnemonic Pegs

A mnemonic is a device, such as a formula or rhyme, used as an aid in remembering. You probably already use simple verbal mnemonics to remember which way to turn a screwdriver ("righty righty, lefty loosey"), which way to adjust a clock for daylight savings time ("spring forward, fall back"), or where notes are placed on a staff of music ("every good boy does fine" and "face" for notes with a treble clef).

The "peg" in each of these mnemonics is a word that serves as both a reminder and a placeholder for an action or item. For instance, "righty tighty" is the peg that reminds us to turn the screwdriver to the right when we want to tighten a screw. Unfortunately, verbal pegs often rely on rhymes ("righty tighty") or words that sound the same but have different meaning ("spring" as an action and "spring" as a season), which makes them difficult to create quickly. Also, while words are the best tool ever invented for communicating, images are the most effective means God has given us for remembering.

In Thomas Aquinas's magnum opus, *Summa Theologica*, the theologian lists "four things whereby a man perfects his memory." The first on his list is creating strong images.

> First, when a man wishes to remember a thing, he should take some suitable yet somewhat unwonted [that is, unusual] illustration of it, since the unwonted strikes us more, and so makes a greater and stronger impression on the mind; and this explains why we remember better what we saw when we were children. Now the reason for the necessity of finding these illustrations or images, is that simple and spiritual impressions easily slip from the mind, unless they be tied as it were to some corporeal image, because human knowledge has a greater hold on sensible objects. For this reason, memory is assigned to the sensitive part of the soul.[3]

In *The Memory Book*, Harry Lorayne and Jerry Lucas offer four simple rules for helping to create such unusual images.

- The rule of substitution—picture one item instead of the other.
- The rule of out of proportion—try to see items as larger than life.
- The rule of exaggeration—embellish or overstate some feature, number, or expression of the image.
- The rule of action—action is always easier to remember than static imagery, so try to incorporate some form of action into an image.[4]

Applying these rules will help us develop one of the most important tools for memorization—the ability to quickly create ridiculous and unusual images.

Linking Image Pegs

The link system is one of the simplest of all memory techniques and connects many of the other techniques we'll use. This method is applied by linking words or images together into a chain by using a sequence of events or simple story.

Notice how in our Ten Commandments example, the sequence of events tied each peg to the next one and helped us remember the order by placing it in a specific context. For short lists, this technique can often be sufficient for your memorization purposes.

The Memory Palace

Next to creating memorable images, the memory palace is the single most effective tool for remembering large amounts of material. The invention of the technique is credited to Simonides of Ceos, a famous fifth-century Greek poet. After performing at a banquet, Simonides stepped outside to meet two men who were waiting for him. But while he was outside the banquet hall, it collapsed, crushing everyone within. The bodies were so disfigured, they could not be identified for proper burial. But Simonides remembered where each guest had been sitting at the table and was able to identify them for burial. This experience suggested to him the principles that were to become central to the later development of the memory palace.

The Roman politician and lawyer Cicero described Simonides's technique in 55 BC.

> [Simonides] inferred that persons desiring to train this faculty (of memory) must select places and form mental images of the things they wish to remember and store those images in the places, so that the order of the places will preserve the order of the things, and the images of the things will denote the things themselves, and we shall employ the places and the images respectively as a wax writing-tablet and the letters written upon it.[5]

Also known as the "method of *loci*," this technique uses an imaginary journey through a sequence of places, or *loci*, each of which acts as a memory link system. For ancient Greeks, the places were often rooms in palaces. But since most of us aren't intimately familiar with the layouts of any palaces, it's preferable to use a location that you already know well, such as your current house or apartment or a childhood home. The key is to choose a memory palace that contains at least ten locations that can be reached in sequence.

The imagined journey through your memory palace might start on the front porch (location 1) and proceed into the foyer (location 2), the living room (location 3), the kitchen (location 4), the dining room (location 5), up the stairs (location 6), into the hall (location 7), into your bathroom (location 8), into your bedroom (location 9), and end in the spare bedroom (location 10).

Choose a journey that matches the actual layout of your house. Imagine walking along this journey, and don't cross over your path or backtrack since this could cause you to miss some locations or use the same ones twice. You can use the same rooms more than once, even on the same list, but be sure to complete the journey before starting again at location 1. (By the way, this practice is said to be the origin of the expressions "in the first place," "in the second place," and so on.)

At you visualize each location, imagine always looking at the scene from the same perspective and looking around the room in the same order, such as from right to left. Practice mentally following your journey and visualizing as much detail as possible. The more details you can see in each location, the more mental hooks you can use to link your image pegs.

Keep in mind that the memory palace is simply the storehouse for the memorable images you create. It provides a structure to help you remember the order and sequence and to prevent you from omitting items. Memorizing each item in a specific location will help to prevent getting items out of order or leaving them out altogether.

Nooks and Crannies

You can expand the capacity of your memory palace without adding extra rooms. Rather than placing only one peg in each location, identify three or four areas—which we'll refer to as nooks—where you can place your images. For instance, if you use your kitchen as a location, you could use the refrigerator, the pantry, and a counter as nooks. Fortunately, your mental images are not limited by space. Don't let that physical constraint concern you. Instead, let your imaginary space expand to fit the object. Identify at least three nooks for every location.

As the author of the famous book on memorization *Rhetorica ad Herennium* noted more than 2,000 years ago, mnemonic images come in two types—one for things (*res*) and the other for words (*verba*). In this chapter, we're focusing on memorizing things (objects). Memorizing words is a bit more difficult and relies more on drill and repetition than on mnemonic devices.

Practice using the tips you've learned to memorize another list of items. Choose a list that suits your interest. For example, a movie buff can practice by memorizing all the Best Picture Oscar winners for the past 20 or 30 years. History buffs can memorize the US presidents or the monarchy of Britain.

Literature buffs can memorize the titles of Shakespeare's plays. The key is to choose a list you are interested in that has 25 to 50 items. You may spend 30 to 60 minutes coming up with the images and putting them in your memory palace. Then practice going through your memory palace and reciting the items in order.

How to Focus

All of humanity's problems," said the Christian philosopher Blaise Pascal, "stem from man's inability to sit quietly in a room alone." Pascal was only slightly exaggerating. Many of the activities that can shape our worldview and improve our lives—such as reading the Bible or memorizing Scripture—require an ability to focus that we often lack.

Focus is the act of concentrating your interest or activity on something. Focus as a habit occurs when we've developed the skill to begin a task without procrastination and then maintain our attention and effort until the task is complete.[1] With time and effort, we can develop this habit and improve our ability to concentrate by regularly applying a few simple methods.

Identify the Distraction

The primary enemy of focus is distraction, which takes three broad forms: external, internal, and intentional.

External distractions occur when the distraction is coming from outside ourselves and is not something we choose. For example, if you're studying and you hear a loud clanging noise coming from outside your window, the external distraction may make it nearly impossible to focus. This type of distraction is often the most annoying, but it tends to be the easiest to overcome in the long term.

Internal distraction occurs when our own brains make it difficult to maintain focus. Some children and adults may have a physical or mental condition that causes internal distraction (about 11 percent of American children age 4 to

17 have been diagnosed with attention-deficit/hyperactivity disorder).[2] But for most of us, internal distraction—such as thoughts that distract us from focusing—occurs because we have not trained our brains to overcome certain emotional states, such as boredom.

Intentional distraction occurs when the distraction is coming from outside ourselves and is something we have chosen. The most common form of intentional distraction is multitasking—dealing with more than one task at the same time. We can multitask, but we cannot *concentrate* on two or more tasks at the same time. This should be obvious, yet the idea that we can divide our concentration and still be effective is one of the most persistent myths in modern life. Despite dozens of psychological studies that show multitasking destroys our focus and makes us less productive, people still refuse to accept that multitasking reduces their ability to be effective.

Understanding which type of distraction is affecting you can help you develop your concentration, and learning to overcome that type of distraction is the key to developing the habit of focus.

Focus Your Focus

Often, we cannot focus on something because we do not choose to give our sustained concentration to only that one thing. Focus requires deciding where and on what you will focus. Make it as specific as possible. Rather than telling yourself, "I need to focus," give yourself a specific imperative, such as "I'm going to focus on closely reading this chapter."

Sleep, Exercise, and Water

Many internal distractions can be caused by physiological conditions, particularly a lack of water (mild dehydration), a lack of sleep, and a lack of physical activity. Getting enough of each is imperative for developing the long-term habit of focus.

Manage Energy, Not Just Time

Internal distraction is more likely to occur when you're tired or otherwise less alert. Oftentimes we waste time on nonproductive activities (like checking social media) when we are most refreshed, such as in the mornings, and we push off tasks that require concentration until later in the day when our energy is waning. Whenever possible, arrange activities that require your concentration during the times when you have the most energy.

Tips for Training Children

Exercise First, Focus Second

"Homework first, play second" has been a mantra since parents began sending their kids to school. But this sequence may set children up for failure since their pent-up energy can create an internal distraction. Adults often have too little energy to perform all we need to accomplish, but children can have an excess of energy that can be as distracting as having a lack of energy. Before giving a child tasks that require sustained focus on cognitive activities, give them time to engage in physical activities (and no, watching television or playing video games doesn't count).

Remove External Distractions

Children, especially adolescents, have a strong preference for intentional distractions. Given the choice, most children would prefer to "study" in front of the television, with music blaring, or while texting their friends—or all three at the same time. And most will swear that it doesn't affect their ability to focus.

The best approach is to physically remove as many external distractions as possible—or physically move the child to an area with a minimal number of distractions. Start this habit as early as possible in the child's life so that a distraction-free environment becomes the norm when they need to focus.

Don't Set Unrealistic Expectations

In 1858, tens of thousands of Americans attended the debates between presidential candidates Abraham Lincoln and Stephen Douglas. The crowds sat and listened as one candidate spoke for an hour, the other candidate spoke for 90 minutes, and the first candidate gave his 30-minute rebuttal. Few of us today have the stamina to sit quietly for three hours, much less to focus that long on a political debate. Our attention spans are more constricted than those of our ancestors, and while we may be able to extend them, we shouldn't set unrealistic expectations for ourselves or our children.

How long should we expect children to sustain high levels of concentration? Attention spans will vary from child to child, but they should be able to progressively sustain longer periods of focus as they get older. A useful rule of thumb is a minimum of 10 minutes for every grade level (30 minutes for third graders, 70 minutes for seventh graders, and 120 minutes for high school seniors).

PART 9

SKILLS AND HABITS FOR MANAGING CONFLICT

How to Handle Conflict

The seventeenth-century political philosopher Thomas Hobbes said the state of mankind without civil society is "nothing else but a mere war of all against all." Hobbes would have been more accurate if he'd said this was the condition of mankind in almost every circumstance. The sad reality is that we are almost always at war with other people, at war with ourselves, and even at war with our God. For us sinners, conflict is what Hobbes would call the "state of nature."

That's the bad news. The good news is that the good news the gospel— frees us from this interminable and inevitable war of all against all. We are free to pursue peace with others, with ourselves, and with God.

This does not mean, though, that we will not have conflicts. As President Ronald Reagan once said, "Peace is not the absence of conflict, but the ability to cope with conflict by peaceful means."[1] Jesus has not freed us from a life of conflict (at least not yet), but he has made it possible for us to deal with conflict peacefully.

Conflict comes in several varieties. For instance, intrapersonal conflict occurs within an individual, while intragroup conflict is a type of conflict that occurs among individuals within a group, such as a church or family (see chapter 45, "How to Handle Family Conflict"). In this chapter we'll focus solely on the most common type of conflict: interpersonal conflict, a conflict between two individuals.

The source of almost all interpersonal conflict is the same: failure to submit to and obey God. If that seems overly broad, ask yourself how many relational conflicts you have observed in which both people are fully submitting and obeying God. You're unlikely to find any instances in which neither person is seeking to get their own way. We seek our own desires rather than what God wants for us, as we learn in the New Testament.

> What causes fights and quarrels among you? Don't they come from your desires that battle within you? You desire but do not have, so you kill. You covet but you cannot get what you want, so you quarrel and fight. You do not have because you do not ask God. When you ask, you do not receive, because you ask with wrong motives, that you may spend what you get on your pleasures (James 4:1-3).

We can sum up three of James's commands under this one head, says Steven J. Cole: Submit to God unconditionally (4:7), draw near to God (4:8), and humble yourself before God (4:10).[2]

This is not what we want to hear, is it? We want to be told how to get the other person to resolve the conflict by conceding we are right and giving us what we want. Sometimes, of course, the proper result will be for the other person to give in, but that is because it is what God deems is right, not because of our situational superiority.

Tips for Training Children

Winning by Losing

Conflict is inevitable, but our goal as Christians is to live in peace. As Paul says, "If it is possible, as far as it depends on you, live at peace with everyone" (Romans 12:18). One of the ways we can make it possible is to avoid unnecessary conflicts.

Sometimes this means refusing to use our own power and authority. When Jesus was faced with violence, he simply walked away (Luke 4:28-30). He could have overpowered anyone who threatened him—and yet he chose to submit to the will of his Father and avoid further confrontation.

Sometimes avoiding unnecessary conflicts means allowing ourselves to be wronged. The best approach to dealing with a minor slight or insult is often to simply forgive it. As Proverbs says, "It is to one's glory to overlook an offense" (19:11).

Some conflicts, however, are both necessary and unavoidable. We don't want to raise children who think, for instance, that they should suffer abuse (or allow others to be abused) simply to avoid conflict. But we need to ensure they understand that sometimes the best way to win at life is not to be afraid to lose at interpersonal conflict.

Negotiation for Younger Children

Every Christian child should be taught the principles of conflict resolution outlined by Jesus (Matthew 5:23-25; 18:15-17). James Jackson offers a short and simple formulation that is easy to teach to kids:

1. *Quickly.* Don't wait for the problem to get worse or escalate. Deal with the problems as quickly as possible.

2. *Face-to-face.* We live in an age where face-to-face communication can be avoided. Whenever possible, though, children should be encouraged to address conflict directly and in person. It's more uncomfortable than sending a text or making a phone call. But we need to teach them relationships are about people, and human engagement (including conflict resolution) was not intended to be mediated solely through electronic means.

3. *One-on-one.* This step may be difficult for smaller children, and in many cases it may require one-on-one-on-one (including an adult). But in general, interpersonal conflicts that do not directly involve a group of other children should be handled between the individual children.

4. *Get help.* Conflict comes naturally for children, but conflict resolution does not. They simply aren't equipped with the interpersonal skills necessary to address most conflicts on their own. While older children, teens, and adults should get help when the conflict can't be resolved, younger children should be taught to get help at the earliest stage. The idea that they can or will work it out on their own is wishful thinking of tired and exasperated parents (for more on this point, see chapter 45, "How to Handle Family Conflict").

Negotiation for Older Children

Older children and teens need to be taught the same process as younger children. They also need advanced instruction on how to avoid conflict. But older kids also have interests that they need to learn to defend or negotiate biblically.

"Having a loving concern for others does not mean always giving in to their demands," says Ken Sande.[3] "We do have a responsibility to look out for our own interests (Philemon 2:4)." In such a situation, Sande recommends using a five-step method of cooperative negotiation that can be summarized by the acronym PAUSE:

- *Prepare*. Pray, get the facts, identify issues and interests, develop options, study relevant Scripture passages, seek godly counsel, and so on.

- *Affirm relationships*. Earnestly seek to understand, allow face-saving, give praise and thanks, and the like.

- *Understand interests*. Identify the other person's concerns, desires, needs, limitations, or fears.

- *Search for creative solutions*. Search for solutions that will satisfy as many interests as possible.

- *Evaluate options objectively and reasonably*. Evaluate possible solutions objectively and reasonably so you can reach the best possible agreement.

How to Deal with Bullying and Harassment

For generations, many Americans—including far too many Christians—considered bullying a normal, albeit unfortunate, part of childhood. But over the past few decades, society has begun to realize that bullying can have long-term effects on everyone involved.

Kids who are bullied can experience depression, anxiety, mood disorders, and reduced academic achievement. Kids who bully others can also engage in violent and other risky behaviors into adulthood. They are more likely to engage in early sexual activity, abuse alcohol and other drugs in adolescence and as adults, and be abusive toward their romantic partners, spouses, or children as adults. And kids who merely *witness* bullying are more likely to...

- Increase their use of tobacco, alcohol, or other drugs
- Experience mental health problems, including depression and anxiety
- Miss or skip school[1]

Because of these harmful effects, understanding bullying and knowing how to address it are important parts of developing a biblical, neighbor-loving worldview.

A Definition

The US Department of Health and Human Services defines bullying as unwanted, aggressive behavior among school-aged children that involves a real or perceived power imbalance. The behavior is repeated, or has the potential to be repeated, over time.

To be considered bullying, the behavior must be aggressive, repeated, and include an imbalance of power between the children. Kids who bully use their power—such as physical strength, access to embarrassing information, or popularity—to control or harm others.[2]

The Types and Modes of Bullying

Bullying can be classified into four types: verbal, social, physical, and damage to property. Verbal bullying is saying or writing something that is cruel or intended to harm, and includes such acts as making inappropriate sexual comments or threatening to cause pain. Social bullying, sometimes referred to as relational bullying, involves hurting someone's reputation or relationships, and includes spreading rumors or causing intentional public embarrassment. Physical bullying involves hurting a person's body and includes such actions as hitting, kicking, spitting, pushing, sexually abusing, or taking one's possessions. The fourth type of bullying involves any type of intentional damage to a child's property.

The two modes of bullying include direct (bullying that occurs in the presence of a child) and indirect (bullying not directly communicated to a targeted child, such as spreading rumors).

Cyberbullying

Because of the prevalence of media technology, children now must deal with electronic bullying, or cyberbullying—bullying that occurs using technology (including but not limited to phones, email, chat rooms, instant messaging, and online posts). Cyberbullying is not a different type of bullying; it just involves an electronic context. Cyberbullying involves some form of verbal bullying (such as threatening or harassing text messages), social bullying (such as spreading rumors online), or damage to property (such as destroying homework files).

The Prevalence of Bullying

About 28 percent of US students in grades 6 to 12 report experiencing bullying. About 30 percent admit to bullying others, and 70.6 percent say they have seen bullying in their schools. Most bullying occurs during the middle school years.

Where Bullying Occurs

Most bullying takes place in school areas, including school playgrounds and buses. One large study revealed the percentage of middle school students who had experienced bullying in these places at school:

> classrooms (29.3 percent)
>
> hallways or lockers (29 percent)
>
> cafeterias (23.4 percent)
>
> gyms or PE classes (19.5 percent)
>
> bathrooms (12.2 percent)
>
> playgrounds or recess (6.2 percent)[3]

Tips for Training Children

Ask Your Child About Bullying

Has your child been bullied? Before you say no, you might want to ask them. Only about 20 to 30 percent of students who are bullied notify adults about the bullying.[4] If the child admits to being bullied, let them know you are on their side. "Realize that your child is not to blame for being bullied, and refuse to believe any lies being told about him or her," says Dr. Walt Larimore. "The bully is the disturbed one. Remind your children of their value in your and God's sight, and help them understand that no one can make them feel inferior without their permission."[5]

Labels That Stigmatize Children

Bullying involves both behavior and power imbalance. When we label a child a bully, we imply their behavior can't change ("that's just what they are"). Similarly, when we label a child a victim, we may be giving the impression the child is weak or inferior. In both cases the labels fail to acknowledge the multiple roles children might play in different bullying situations. A child who bullies may also be the victim of bullying by other children.

Instead of labeling the children involved, focus on the behavior. For instance, rather than calling a child a bully, refer to them as a child who bullied. Instead of labeling a child as a victim, refer to them as a child who was bullied. And instead of calling a child a bully/victim, refer to them as a child who was both bullied and bullied others.[6]

The Circle of Bullying

Even if your child is not bullying or being bullied, they may be in the broader group known as the circle of bullying. The Olweus Bullying Prevention Program identifies several roles kids play regarding bullying:

- Students who bully
- Students who are bullied
- Followers or henchmen—those who participate but do not start the bullying
- Supporters or passive bullies—those who support the bullying but do not take an active part
- Passive supporters or possible bullies—those who like the bullying but do not display open support
- Disengaged onlookers—spectators who don't take a stand
- Possible defenders—those who dislike the bullying and think they ought to help but don't act
- Defenders—opponents of bullying who try to help the bullied student

Encourage Intervention

We should teach our children to be defenders and not to be afraid to protect other people (Matthew 7:12; 1 Thessalonians 5:14; Hebrews 13:6). Their willingness to intervene can make a significant difference. Research has shown that more than half the time (57 percent), when children intervene and play the role of "defender," bullying stops within ten seconds.[7]

Rules to Remember and Live By

Rather than waiting until an incident occurs, teach your child beforehand how they are expected to behave as a defender. At a minimum, children should be told to always follow these rules:

- I will not bully others.
- I will try to help other children who are bullied.
- I will try to include other children who are left out.
- If I know that somebody is being bullied, I will tell an adult at school and my parents.
- I will pray both for those who are being bullied and those who are bullying others.

How to Handle Family Conflict

The oldest type of human conflict is family conflict. It started when Adam blamed his wife, Eve, for his disobedience (Genesis 3:12), continued with one of their sons murdering his sibling (Genesis 4:8), and affected just about every major character in the Bible. Even Jesus had to deal with conflicts with his own family (Mark 3:21).

"The early chapters of Genesis explain that the brokenness of nearly every facet of family life stems from God's judgment against our first parents," says Richard Pratt Jr.

> No family is "fine," "without problems," or "great" until someone destroys it. Every home is broken from the day it begins. If you and I were to believe what the Bible says about the origins of our family problems, our attitudes and actions would be very different. We would be more sympathetic with others going through hard times, more vigilant about keeping our own families on track, and more devoted to pursuing help from God rather than simply assigning blame. Wouldn't that be a welcome change?[1]

The first and most essential step for learning the habit of handling family conflict is to constantly remind ourselves that our homes are broken because we are all sinners. We should expect conflict among sinners who are confined to the same space and forced to interact with each other the first decades of their lives. This is why children have more conflict with their siblings than they do with their friends. As Scottish researcher Samantha Punch points out, siblings will be there tomorrow, no matter what. "Sibship is a relationship in which the boundaries of social interaction can be pushed to the limit," says Punch. "Rage and irritation need not be suppressed, whilst politeness and toleration can be neglected."[2]

Fortunately, while we've inherited the tradition of family conflict from Adam and Eve, we've also inherited the biblical tradition of how to handle conflicts within the family. You cannot completely break the cycle, but you can teach your children to handle dissension in a way that will affect not only your immediate family but also your children's extended family. It may even affect the family line for generations.

The most important tool for handling family conflict is to keep your focus on Christ and to constantly search his Word to understand his commands for you and your family. But you should keep certain principles in mind as you develop within yourself and your children the habit of dealing faithfully with family conflicts.

Know Your Roles

Conflict inevitably arises when we try to subvert or avoid the roles God has given us in the family. We should know and understand the familial responsibilities the Bible outlines for husbands and fathers (Ephesians 5:25-33; 6:4; Colossians 3:19,21; 1 Peter 3:7), wives and mothers (Ephesians 5:22-24; Colossians 3:18; 1 Peter 3:1-6), and children (Ephesians 6:1-3; Colossians 3:20). Commit yourself and your children to obeying God's commands for how you should relate to one another.

Secondary Sources of Conflict

All conflict is ultimately rooted in sin, for if we loved one another as Christ loves us, there would be no source of interpersonal conflict. But most all forms of family conflict have a secondary source that drives and fuels the division. For example, a child may be cruel to their sibling because they crave parental attention—even if it's negative attention. By looking at patterns of misbehavior, we may discover a source that we can deal with to mitigate the problem.

Avoid Favoritism

One secondary source of conflict is so harmful, it is worth addressing specifically—parental favoritism. In the book of Genesis, we see several intra-family conflicts driven by parental favoritism. For example, Isaac and Rebekah each showed favoritism toward their twin sons: "Isaac, who had a taste for wild game, loved Esau, but Rebekah loved Jacob" (Genesis 25:28). And when he had children of his own, Jacob (also known as Israel) favored his son Joseph: "Now Israel loved Joseph more than any of his other sons" (Genesis 37:3). This favoritism caused sinful divisiveness that plagued both families.

Favoritism also can have negative effects on our children today, as Ilan Shrira and Joshua D. Foster explain:

> Disfavored children experience worse outcomes across the board: more depression, greater aggressiveness, lower self-esteem, and poorer academic performance. These repercussions are far more extreme than any benefits the favored children get out of it (negative things just have a stronger impact on people than positive things). And it's not all rosy for the favored children either—their siblings often come to resent them, poisoning those relationships.
>
> Many of these consequences persist long after children have grown up and moved out of the house. People don't soon forget that they were disfavored by their parents, and many people report that being disfavored as a child continues to affect their self-esteem and their relationships in adulthood.[3]

We may show favoritism and not even realize it. Rather than rely on our own subjective impression, we should ask our spouse, friends, or extended family where we exhibit signs of loving one child more than our others. Don't be defensive if they point out how you are partial. Instead, strive to be as impartial in your relations with your children as you would be with any other member of the body of Christ (James 2:9).

The Duties of Fellowship

We often use the term "fellowship" in its colloquial sense of an association of persons having similar interests. And at times we do, regrettably, engage in fellowship only at that most basic level. The term, though, has a much richer meaning in the New Testament—a meaning that can apply to our fellowship with our Christian children.

Scripture makes it clear that we have fellowship with other Christians because we first have fellowship with Christ (1 John 1:3). If our children are believers, we are connected to them not only through the parental bond but also through our union with Christ. We are their mother or father in the flesh as well as their brother or sister in Christ. This means we need to be careful when approaching our conflicts with our children.

When embroiled in conflict, we must ask ourselves whether it is an issue we should address as parent to a child or as one believer to another. In other words, do we deal with the conflict from a position of authority or on a more equal setting, as we would in fellowship with other believers outside our family? The categories (parental and fellowship) aren't mutually exclusive, of course, and they may overlap in ways that make it difficult to determine which to apply. But by recognizing we are not just dealing with our child but with a fellow believer, we can gain a clearer perspective on the conflict.

Tips for Training Children

Parental Intervention

Do you have two or more young children? Do they seem to constantly be in conflict? It's not your imagination. Research has shown that when siblings between the ages of three and seven are together, they clash an average of three and a half times per hour. The studies found that on average, those fights lasted a total of 10 minutes out of every 60.[4] So during the day (12 hours of interaction), your children are likely to be in conflict for the equivalent of two hours!

Dealing with such conflicts can be emotionally draining, so many parents prefer to stand aside and let their children try to work it out. But children under the age of seven haven't developed the conflict-resolution skills they need to do this.

Afshan A. Siddiqui and Hildy S. Ross investigated 40 families on two occasions. Each family included two children who were studied when they were two and a half and four and a half years old, and two years later, at four and a half and six and a half years. They observed four types of conflict endings in sibling conflicts: compromise, reconciliation, submission, and no resolution. At both ages, conflicts typically ended with no resolution. Submission was the second-most common, compromise was third, and reconciliation was least common. As the children got older, submissions decreased and no resolutions increased, while no changes were observed in either compromise or reconciliation.

However, when parents intervened, there was a greater likelihood of conflicts ending in compromise or reconciliation. Interventions led directly to a resolution only 16 percent of time. But in nearly half the times in which parents intervened (42 percent), the children ultimately resolved the conflicts themselves and ended more often with no resolution and less often with children's submission to their siblings.[5]

Having less than half the conflicts end in no resolution may not seem all that encouraging. But what it shows is that young children simply do not have the tools necessary to resolve their own conflicts. Laurie Kramer, a professor of applied family studies at the University of Illinois, says children under eight are generally unable to manage conflicts with their siblings on their own. "The research that I and others have done," said Kramer, "has clearly shown that for children who don't already have those skills in conflict management, it is critical for parents to step in and help."[6]

4 Steps to Conflict Resolution

These five steps are helpful for training younger children.

1. *Enforce a cool-down period.* Before attempting to address the conflict, have the children cool down emotionally by separating from one another or being silent. After even a few minutes of a cool-down period, young children tend to be less emotionally invested in the conflict.

2. *Have each side explain how they contributed to the conflict.* If most young children are to be believed, they are usually sitting quietly, minding their own business, when—out of nowhere and for no reason—their sibling violates the norms of civil society by punching them, calling them names, or stealing their toys. The reality, of course, is that the supposedly innocent victim usually did something to provoke or escalate the conflict. And even when they did nothing ahead of time, they contributed to it once the conflict erupted. As Proverbs says, "He who tells his story first makes people think he is right, until the other comes to test him" (Proverbs 18:17 NLV).

Require each child to be honest about their involvement, and let them know that "I didn't do anything" was only believable the first thousand times you heard it from them. Remind them that "People may be right in their own eyes, but the LORD examines their heart" (Proverbs 21:2 NLT) and ask them to be honest about what God is seeing in their heart.

3. *Seek mutual understanding.* Once they've owned up to their responsibility, they can then be heard and their feelings can be understood, if not vindicated. "For this phase, you have each participant take a turn sharing something they want the other(s) to know," says Elaine Shpungin, the director of the University of Illinois Psychological Services Center, "followed by the Listener saying back their understanding of the message. I like to start with the person I believe is least able to listen (sometimes due to age, sometimes due to how upset they are)."[7]

4. *Agree on an action plan.* Once each child has owned up to their role in the conflict and had an opportunity to be heard, ask them to come up with an action plan for moving forward. The simpler the solution, the better, for it's more likely to be remembered and implemented. For example, instead of telling them, "Don't hit your brother," let them determine a positive alternative.

In following the steps outlined above, try to keep the process as simple as possible. You're probably going to have to deal with conflicts on average about once an hour every day for at least a decade. Don't make more work for yourself than is necessary.

Private and Public Methods of Conflict Resolution

Require that older children follow the biblical pattern of conflict resolution. Private resolution includes steps to resolve the conflict directly and privately with the other family member. The first step is to consider whether they should simply squash the conflict by overlooking the offense (Proverbs 19:11). If it's too serious to ignore, they should go to the person and attempt to resolve it amicably (Matthew 18:15). (For more suggestions, see chapter 43, "How to Handle Conflict.")

If the conflict cannot be resolved privately, require that they widen the circle by asking one or two more people (usually a parent) to serve as witnesses and mediators. After this step, if the conflict continues and involves a matter of sin, then other members of the church need to be brought in to seek a resolution.

By requiring both an informal and formal process, you help children resolve conflicts and show them that God takes such division in the home seriously.

46

How to Handle Peer Pressure

Peer pressure is the feeling that one must do the same things as other people of one's age and social group to be liked or respected by them.[1] All of us are subjected to peer pressure in both positive and negative ways and in subtle and overt manners. The influence of our peer groups leads us to conform to social norms and ultimately helps us develop our sense of self and our place in society.

During the early adolescent through late teen years, children become more aware of a desire to fit in and find their niche in society. This makes them more susceptible to the positive and negative influences of peer pressure. But parents can play a powerful role in shaping these peer interactions.

Know Their Peer Group

The most important and obvious step a parent can take is to help their child select the right group of peers. For better and for worse, your child will be influenced by the people they associate with. The Bible doesn't use the term "peer pressure," but it has quite a lot to say about the company we keep and avoiding negative influences: "Walk with the wise and become wise, for a companion of fools suffers harm" (Proverbs 13:20). "My son, if sinful men entice you, do not give in to them" (Proverbs 1:10). "Do not be misled: 'Bad company corrupts good character'" (1 Corinthians 15:33). We can't completely control whom they will be exposed to, of course, but whenever possible, a parent should know their child's peers. And as much as we can, we should choose whom they will spend their time with.

Intergenerational Influences

One of the most unfortunate realities of the modern era is that children spend too much time with children. Outside of parents and teachers, most teens and children do not associate with older people daily. Unfortunately, this is often true even in our churches, which tend to be voluntarily segregated by age groups.

Intergenerational community is part of God's vision for the church, which is why we—and our children—need friendships that cross generational lines. Having older "peers" in their life can dilute the effect of their own age cohorts and give teens a broader perspective on life. It is also helpful for older children and teens to have an adult in the church (and outside their family) they can turn to for guidance or to talk to about their struggles.

Peer Problems for Parents

While helping to select our child's friends and associates is one of the most effective steps we can take for limiting negative peer groups, we should avoid three dangers.

1. *The bad-company project.* In our attempt to be caring and compassionate, we may put our children in relational danger. A prime example is when we encourage our child to befriend children whom the apostle Paul would deem to be "bad company." We justify the relationship by telling ourselves that our child will be a positive and perhaps even godly influence on their wayward neighbor. But we Christian parents tend to overestimate our children's moral influence and leadership abilities. Instead of being a role model, our children may be the ones who are enticed to sin.

If you encourage such friendships, try to encourage settings where other Christian adults or children are also present (such as youth group) and avoid private, one-on-one encounters.

2. *The Eddie Haskell effect.* The popular television sitcom *Leave It to Beaver* (1958 to 1965) featured a recurring character named Eddie Haskell, who "has become a cultural reference, recognized as an archetype for insincere sycophants."[2] When adults were around, Eddie was ingratiating and polite. But when adults were not in the room, Eddie would show his true character as a bullying, conniving jerk.

When you were a teenager, you probably knew people like Eddie. They were well liked by parents only because parents didn't know what horrible influences they were. How can we avoid falling for the new generation of Eddie Haskells?

The easiest way is usually to spend plenty of time around our child's peers. Teens who are two-faced often have trouble hiding their true natures for long. By being around your child's friends in various settings and circumstances, you can often gain a better understanding of their character.

Another approach is to simply ask other children or teens what the suspected Eddie is really like. If their experience is markedly different from your own, it could be a red flag.

3. *The online-only friend.* You should know whom your children are associating with, which is why they should never have friends they only know from online interactions. This may seem like a harsh rule—and a difficult one to enforce—but the danger of negative peer influences rises exponentially online. If possible, set the rules for online engagement early in your child's life so that when they are older, abstaining from online-only friendships will be the established norm.

Tips for Training Children

The Five Years Prior to "No"

Peer pressure tends to be something parents address when a child reaches early or late adolescence. That's when we begin telling them they should say no to various temptations to engage in sinful or inappropriate behavior. The problem is that this is usually the time when parental influence is on the wane and peer influence is on the rise.

Rather than waiting until they are under pressure, begin laying the groundwork about five years before they can be expected to deal with an issue. This may lead to some awkward conversations (such as talking to your ten-year-old girl about sex and drugs), but by planting the seed early, you can shape how they'll respond later in life.

Clear Signals

Your kids need you to send them clear signals about what types of behavior are inappropriate. This should be obvious, but it's shocking how often

Christian parents inadvertently encourage negative peer influences by undermining their own values. For example, some parents allow teens to drink alcohol at home, claiming, "I'd rather they drink under my roof, where I can watch them, than do it somewhere else." The result is that these underage minors will drink alcohol at home—and anywhere else they can. This is the message they are getting from their parent: "There's nothing wrong with underage drinking; just be safe about it."

Instead, we should be clear and consistent in our disapproval. Sending clear signals is almost always more effective than trying to carve out exceptions. For example, a survey by Mothers Against Drunk Driving found that teens whose parents told them underage drinking is completely unacceptable are 80 percent less likely to drink, compared with those whose parents give their teens other messages about drinking.[3]

Give Them a Plan

What will your child say if they are encouraged to engage in certain behaviors, such as taking drugs? The truth is, you probably don't know. You may have given them vague suggestions or recommended the generic "just say no." But unless you have talked to them in detail about how they'll respond, you can't really know what they'll say when the time comes.

Consider role-playing common peer-pressure situations. Your teen will likely find such practice cheesy, annoying, and a bit embarrassing. But the practice will be beneficial, as they are likely to realize when they are faced with the real-life scenarios. They may not enjoy these conversations with Mom or Dad, but knowing they're armed with the right words to say can be secretly comforting for them.

Be Their Backup

The risk of giving in to peer pressure can be compounded when the child has already engaged in forbidden behavior. For example, if they snuck out to go to a party and the person they rode with is pressuring them to drink, they may feel they have no other choice but to join in. Reduce that pressure by letting them know you are their means of escape. Make sure they know they can contact you whenever they are in an uncomfortable or dangerous situation and you'll always come get them. This doesn't mean they shouldn't suffer the consequences of their misbehavior, of course. But they should understand that the repercussions will be lighter than if they hadn't come to you to save them from further danger or harm.

Focus on Jesus

Help your child truly understand that Jesus is not just watching what they do, but that, as a believer, they are united with Christ (2 Corinthians 4:10). Remind them, as Paul says, "Do you not realize that Christ Jesus is in you?" (2 Corinthians 13:5). And as John wrote, "Whoever claims to live in him must live as Jesus did" (1 John 2:6). Because they are in Jesus and Jesus is in them, they are accepted by one greater than any of their peers, and they are connected with one who has the power to overcome any pressure.

PART 10

SKILLS AND HABITS FOR EVANGELISM

47

How to Start a Conversation About the Gospel

When we give our life to Christ, we are made ambassadors for a kingdom. We are given not only good news to share with others but also one of the most powerful communication tools ever developed—the conversation.

A conversation is simply a form of interactive, spontaneous communication between people who are following unspoken rules of discourse in an agreeable and polite manner. Starting conversations about the gospel is often difficult because of the common dictum that we should avoid talking about money, politics, and religion.[1]

We need to ensure we don't pass along such prejudices to our children. Some people are in fact uncomfortable talking about religious ideas and issues, but many, if not most, have a genuine interest in spiritual matters. That's certainly true for Christians, because every believer came to the faith because someone talked to them about Jesus. Similarly, millions of people are members of non-Christian faiths or are "spiritual but not religious." They too are likely to have an interest in discussing religion.

When Jesus encountered the woman at the well (John 4), he demonstrated that conversations can be powerful tools for revealing his identity and his kingdom. We can help our kids unlock the power of gospel conversations by teaching and modeling the following techniques.

Be Open to Conversation

When he sat at the well, Jesus was likely tired and parched and in no mood to talk. But when he encountered the Samaritan woman, he knew his mission was to "finish [the] work" he had been sent by the Father to do (John 4:34). Being like Jesus doesn't mean we must have a conversation with every stranger we meet or that we can't enjoy quiet time alone. But we should generally be open to such encounters, and we should teach our children to be open to the Spirit's prompting to start a conversation about the gospel.

Be Interested in People

People like to talk about what they know. And the one thing they know better than anything else is themselves. People aren't necessarily being narcissistic for wanting to talk about themselves; they may just want to talk about what they know with someone who appears interested. By teaching children to be interested in others, we prepare them to love and serve their neighbors.

Ask Questions but Don't Interrogate

When talking to people about faith issues, we need to show genuine interest by asking people about themselves. Don't just rattle off a series of questions, but listen closely and ask follow-up questions based on their responses to previous questions. The goal is to make the other person feel they are being heard, not that they are being interrogated.

Uncover Their Burden

At some point in a conversation, a person is likely to relate an experience they are going through. A simple way to establish empathy and signal concern and care is to respond with some variation of "that sounds challenging." Almost everyone believes they are going through something difficult or unappreciated or that their life is burdensome in some way. The challenges in their life can provide an opening to discuss spiritual matters.

"May I Pray for You?"

If a person is willing to reveal a burden, ask if you can pray for them. When you ask, though, the reason should be because you are truly interested in interceding to God on their behalf. It's not a technique to turn the conversation, though it can help you gauge a person's interest in talking more about the gospel. If it seems appropriate, you can then follow up with questions like these:

Do you think much about spiritual matters?

Does faith play a significant role in your life?

What do you think about God?

Listen Carefully to Their Responses

You don't have to agree with them, but avoid trying to show why they are wrong. Show them you are interested in their views, opinions, and concerns. Demonstrate that you're not merely waiting to explain to them what you believe.

"The Reason I Ask..."

After broaching a spiritual topic and listening to their answers, you can transition by saying, "The reason I ask is..." and then explain why you think talking about Jesus is important. This is your opportunity to share the gospel, though you might find it easier to begin by briefly sharing your own testimony of giving your life to Christ. However, remember that your eyewitness testimony of the power of Jesus, while important, is not the gospel. You don't want to open the door for a discussion about the gospel only to forget the most important part of the conversation.

48

How to Defend the Faith

When we defend the faith, we engage apologetics, the field of theology that uses reason, evidence, and argumentation to respond to objections to Christianity. Tim Keller offers this explanation:

> Apologetics is an answer to the "why" question after you've already answered the "what" question. The what question, of course, is, "What is the gospel?" But when you call people to believe in the gospel and they ask, "Why should I believe that?"—then you need apologetics.[1]

Many verses in the Bible call us to defend the faith (including 2 Corinthians 10:5; 2 Timothy 4:2; Titus 1:9; Jude 1:3), but the one cited most often is 1 Peter 3:15. This verse is often paraphrased as, "Always be prepared to make a defense to anyone who asks you for a reason for the hope that is in you." But to effectively defend the faith we need to use this verse in its full context:

> In your hearts revere Christ as Lord. Always be prepared to give an answer to everyone who asks you to give the reason for the hope that you have. But do this with gentleness and respect, keeping a clear conscience, so that those who speak maliciously against your good behavior in Christ may be ashamed of their slander (1 Peter 3:15-16).

Paul Rezkalla calls this the "Great Commission for apologetics" and notes that it gives us three commands.

1. Set apart Christ as Lord in your heart.

2. Be ready to give an answer to anyone who asks you to give the reason for the hope within you.

3. Do this with gentleness and respect.[2]

Set Apart Christ as Lord

Before we can adequately defend the faith, we must set apart Christ as Lord in our hearts. "To 'set apart' Christ as Lord means to acknowledge that he holds the reins in every area of our lives," says Rezkalla. "We ought to dedicate and consecrate our hearts for God, making Jesus the Lord of our desires, motives, inadequacies—all of who we are. This makes our apologetic more than a mere intellectual exercise; it's an opportunity to defend the hope we have within us."

Of course, the core of the apologetic task is to "be prepared to give an answer to everyone who asks you to give the reason for the hope that you have." Here are three steps you can teach your child to make the task easier.

Ask a Question

When confronted with challenges to the faith, we tend to have one of two reactions. If we know how to answer, we want to respond with a "data dump," blurting out a lengthy response or rebuttal. If we don't know the answer, we may freeze up or become defensive. But there's a better approach—simply ask a question. For instance, if someone claims, "All religions are the same," we can ask, "What do you mean by that? In what ways are all religions the same?"

By asking a question rather than data-dumping or giving them answers, you let the skeptic come to their own conclusions—and perhaps agree with you. This is a tactic Jesus often used when confronting the Pharisees.

One of the most versatile and helpful questions you can ask is, "What do you mean by that?" Gregory Koukl explains why:

> People don't know what they mean much of the time. Often they're merely repeating slogans. When you ask them to flesh out their concern, opinion, or point of view with more precision, they're struck mute. They are forced to think, maybe for the first time, about exactly what they do mean.[3]

Apply What You Know…

Before a child can defend the faith, they have to know about the faith. They may not know as much as an adult who has been a Christian for decades, but they likely know quite a lot about the faith already—more than you may realize. But it's particularly helpful if the child is armed with some Bible verses to include in their responses.

For example, after asking what a person means when they say all religions are the same, the next response could be, "I'm not sure how that could be true. Didn't Jesus say, 'I am the way, and the truth, and the life. No one comes to the Father except through me' (John 14:6)?" By merely applying the relevant information they already have, children can clear up many of the misconceptions and concerns people have about Christianity.

…But Don't Fake It

Your child should never pretend to know an answer if they are unsure, or water down the truth to make it more palatable. Many a believer has done tremendous harm by helping skeptics trade one falsehood for another. A Christian child should be prepared to answer some of the most basic and common objections to the faith, but they should also know how much harm can be done if they confuse people by giving them unreliable answers.

Follow Up with Clarification

Here is a 14-word secret weapon for defending the faith: "I don't know the answer, but I'll find out and get back to you."

This simple sentence is effective for three reasons. First, it shows we are truly interested in answering the person's questions rather than merely trying to win a debate. Second, it removes some of the pressure and buys the child time to research a relevant and accurate response (which increases their knowledge and prepares them to answer the question in the future). Third, it prevents them from wasting their time and casting their "pearls before swine" (Matthew 7:6 kjv). If the person isn't interested in a follow-up answer, they weren't registering a true objection and likely aren't open to hearing more about the faith.

Make sure your child knows they can come to you to help research the answers to their questions. They should also see this 14-word secret weapon in action when they ask you questions about the faith you are unable to answer.

Gentleness and Respect

Many immature Christians are drawn to apologetics because they like to argue. They will spend countless hours online and in person debating hardcore atheists over the most trivial of issues. (I've wasted countless hours doing this myself.) Too often their motives are not godly, and they are more interested in winning an argument about creationism or eschatology than they are in glorifying their Creator.

This biblical command to defend the faith with gentleness and respect requires that we take the other person's arguments and questions seriously, listen to their views charitably, and respond to them lovingly.

49

How to Tell a Bible Story

In the books of Acts we find a story about Stephen facing the Sanhedrin, the supreme court and legislative body in Judea during the Roman period. He has been called to answer charges that he's used blasphemous words against Moses and against God. Stephen could have attempted to defend himself, but instead, he does something that Jews often did but that may seem unusual to readers today—he tells a story from the Bible.

Stephen gives a survey of Old Testament history from Abraham to David, highlighting Israel's pattern of constantly resisting and rejecting its God-appointed leaders. The reason he uses this history is to show how this pattern of rejection in the past foreshadows the ultimate rejection of God's appointed Messiah in the present.[1]

Stephen was using a technique that is now often referred to as biblical storying, the intentional and uninterrupted sharing of God's Word primarily as stories.[2] Storying is a useful method for anyone who wants to engage and communicate God's Word. But it can be an especially powerful tool for children and teens who are learning how to share their faith with their peers.

Here are a few tips to help them get started with the practice of telling a Bible story.

Learn the Story

Choose a story. Choose a story from the Bible that has a special resonance with the child. The more invested they are in the story, the easier it will be for them to follow the steps necessary to learn to tell the story on their own.

Learn the story. Have the child read the Bible story aloud five to ten times. Then test them by having them recite as much of it as they can from memory.

Review the recitation. Make note of what the child missed in their retelling. Did they leave out essential points or significant details? Encourage the child by reminding them that forgetting details is to be expected the first few times they tell the story.

Practice, practice, practice. Have the child spread their practice sessions over several days or weeks so they don't get overwhelmed. But remind them it will take effort. The best storytellers hone their craft through practice.

Use their imagination. Once the child is able to tell the story without leaving out any essential points, have them use their imagination to fill in the narrative and sensory details. They shouldn't embellish the story in a way that would change its meaning, of course. But the child can be encouraged to create vivid images of the scene and setting of the story. For example, in the story about Zacchaeus (Luke 19), the "small in stature" tax collector climbed a sycamore tree so that he could see Jesus. In retelling this story, the child is free to describe the tree in a way that adds color to the story.

Record and analyze. Once they are able to recite the story from memory, make an audio recording and carefully scrutinize the content with them. Are they clearly communicating key biblical truths? Is the story too long? Does it include too many distracting details?

Practice, practice, practice (again). Spend sufficient time practicing telling the story. Once they've sufficiently memorized the story, have them work on the delivery, focusing on the variation in tone and inflection.

Combine it with other stories. Use the same process to learn other Bible stories, and fit them into a chronological storytelling format.

Telling the Story

Start with a prayer. Whether aloud with their audience or silently to themselves, have them say a prayer that the Holy Spirit will help them tell it accurately and compellingly and that the hearts of the hearers will be opened.

Set the opening context. A standard opening line will help both your child and their audience know they are transitioning into the story. Have them use an obvious opening such as, "Now here is a story from God's Word."

Recreate the story. When telling the story to an audience, they may get nervous and forget to include the details that set the scene. Prod them to use vivid imagery. Show them how to include emotion and variation in their voice and to use gestures for emphasis.

Pace the story. Dialogue slows a story; action speeds it up. Have them use pauses to underline main points. Show them how to maintain variety in the pacing.[3]

Have a clear ending. Help them choose an ending line that bookends their opening. For instance, you can conclude by saying, "And that's the end of the story from God's Word." Having a clear opening and ending can help provide a framing device and can prevent the child from feeling awkward about not knowing how to end the story.

Interpret and follow up. After the story, encourage them to interpret and explain the lesson of the story. Have them ask questions of the audience to verify that the listeners understand it and know how to apply it to their own lives. Reply according to listeners' responses by confirming correct answers, removing doubts, and clearing up misunderstandings.[4]

This process gives a child a nonthreatening way to talk about their faith and share it with others. Biblical storytelling not only teaches them valuable communication skills but also helps the child prepare for other helpful spiritual disciplines, such as Bible memorization and meditating on Scripture.

50

How to Share the Gospel

Evangelism is the verbal proclamation of the good news of salvation in Christ, a call for unbelievers to repent and give God the glory for regeneration and conversion.

Know the Core Elements of the Gospel

You can't share the message of the gospel if you don't know what it is. This may seem obvious, but it's surprising how many Christians are unable to clearly explain the basics of the gospel. As Don Whitney says,

> Despite the fact that by their own admission [Christians] have read or heard countless presentations of the Gospel and claim to have experienced new life in Christ through its power, they are unable to convey even the ABCs of the message of salvation.[1]

What exactly is the gospel? Simon Gathercole identifies three aspects of the gospel found in the New Testament.[2]

1. Who Jesus is, especially his identity as royal Messiah and Son of God

2. Jesus's work of atonement and justification accomplished in the cross and resurrection

3. Jesus's work of new creation and of rescue from the power of sin

According to Paul, the gospel is an affirmation of who Jesus is (Romans 1:3-4) and of what he has done (1 Corinthians 15). You should be able to articulate the gospel in a way that includes all three of these elements. Here's an example you can use:

> At its briefest, the gospel is the good news about Jesus Christ: that he is the Son of God and became man for us, that he died in order to restore us to our relationship with God, and that he was raised from the dead and established as Lord over all things.

Or in even fewer words, "The gospel is God's account of his saving activity in Jesus the Messiah, in which, by Jesus's death and resurrection, he atones for sin and brings a new creation."

Before we outline ways to share the gospel, we should first consider the matter of timing. When exactly should you share the gospel with someone? A general rule of thumb is to share the gospel when you're ready.

This answer should help alleviate the pressure you feel to blurt out the gospel to every stranger you encounter on the street. But it should not be used as an excuse to completely avoid sharing God's good news. John Piper offers this suggestion:

> Test yourself to see whether or not Jesus is really precious to you, and whether you believe this person is really lost without him and that it would be the best thing in the world for them to know this, believe this, and be redeemed by this. And if you really believe that, then probably sooner rather than later you're going to find some way to share this with the person that you know.[3]

Once you can explain the gospel and you feel the timing is right, what is the best way to share the good news? Start a conversation and ask questions. (See chapter 47, "How to Start a Conversation About the Gospel.")

Many Christians never share the gospel because they think they don't know the proper methods and techniques of evangelism. They assume they need to have memorized a five-point method or be able to draw illustrations on a napkin to explain the concepts. But all you really need is the ability to carry on a conversation.

Know the Next Steps

After you share the gospel, you are likely to be met by three types of response.

The first reaction is rejection or complete disinterest—they don't want to accept Jesus or continue talking to you about the gospel. Don't be discouraged, for you have done your duty. "We don't fail in our evangelism if we faithfully tell the gospel to someone who is not converted," says Mark Dever, "we fail only if we don't faithfully tell the gospel at all."[4]

The second reaction is continued interest. They may not be ready to respond to this good news, but they are willing to keep talking about it. Ask them if they'd be willing to talk about the topic in the future and if you can answer any questions they have about Jesus. Then do your homework and prepare for the next encounter.

The third reaction is that after hearing the gospel they ask the most important question in the world: "What must I do to be saved?" (Acts 16:30). The reason we proclaim the gospel is to lead an unbeliever to ask that very question, so we should be prepared with a simple answer: "Repent and believe in the good news" (Mark 1:15). That is the heart of what the sinner needs to know to be saved. Shane Raynor recommends keeping the message to the essentials:

> Repent, believe, confess. Keep it simple. There's no need to get bogged down in atonement theory or in trying to explain in detail how everything works. Stick with the basics. The deep theological discussions can come later.[5]

Repent of their sins, and believe and confess that Jesus is Lord and that God has raised him from the dead (Romans 10:10). That is the response that will change their life.

Tips for Training Children

Simplify but Don't Skimp

Once you have a solid grasp on the three elements that comprise the gospel, you'll be better able to help your child create a simple formulation that doesn't leave out any necessary parts. You can even have them directly incorporate the three-part structure in a question-and-answer format.

What is the gospel? The gospel is the good news that...

1. Jesus is the Messiah, the Son of God who

2. died on the cross and rose again to pay for our sins so that

3. we will be with him forever and ever.

Rely on Repetition

Like adults, children will have trouble remembering these core elements. Repetition is therefore essential to help them express the gospel. Quiz them frequently. Ask them to clearly state each element and then have them explain in their own words what it means to them.

Use Role-Play

When the child can remember and explain the gospel, they can also learn how to bring it up in conversation. Role-play conversations with them to show them how to transition to spiritual topics and respond to various reactions. The approach for children and adults will be the same, though children can often be more direct and blunt. A child sharing the gospel with another child may be more comfortable simply asking, "Do you believe in Jesus?" or "Do you know Jesus died for you?"

Beginner Theologians

When teaching children to share the gospel, we need to avoid two extremes. The first is assuming they can't truly understand the good news about Jesus. The Lord said, "Let the little children come to me, and do not hinder them, for the kingdom of God belongs to such as these" (Mark 10:14). Rely on Jesus to determine how much they can come to know him at each age.

The second extreme to avoid is expecting young children to grasp the depths and nuances of the gospel. The goal is to plant a seed of knowledge that will grow as they mature. As they grow in Christ, these beginner theologians will be able to build on the knowledge you equipped them with in their youth.

Recommended Resources

Children's Bibles

There is probably no category of Bibles where the quality varies as widely as children's Bibles. As Rachel Tiemeyer from *Thriving Home* says, "It's important to use discernment when selecting a children's Bible. Remember, these are just storybooks, not the verbatim inspired Word of God. And humans are prone to error."[1] Tiemeyer says we should look for four characteristics in a children's Bible: God-centered, not man-centered; grace-centered, not moralistic; well-written; and containing good illustrations. Here are a few that meet all four criteria.

The Rhyme Bible Storybook for Toddlers by L.J. Sattgast (Zonderkidz, 2014), 40-page board book, infants through age 2

Read Aloud Bible Stories by Ella K. Lindvall (Moody, 1982), 160 pages, ages 2–5

The Rhyme Bible Storybook by Linda Sattgast (Zonderkidz, 2012), 344 pages, ages 4–8

The Big Picture Story Bible by David R. Helm (Crossway, 2014), 465 pages, ages 3–7

The Jesus Storybook Bible by Sally Lloyd-Jones (Zonderkidz, 2007), 352 pages, ages 3–8

ESV Seek & Find Bible (Crossway, 2010), 1,888 pages, ages 6–8

Mighty Acts of God: A Family Bible Story Book by Starr Meade (Crossway, 2010), 288 pages, ages 8–12

The Action Bible by Doug Mauss (David C. Cook, 2010), 752 pages, ages 9–11

NIV Adventure Bible (Lawrence O. Richards, Zonderkidz), 1,488 pages, ages 8–12

The Biggest Story: How the Snake Crusher Brings Us Back to the Garden by Kevin DeYoung (Crossway, 2015), 132 pages, ages 9–12

Bible Handbooks

What the Bible Is All About Handbook for Kids: Bible Handbook for Kids by Henrietta C. Mears (Tyndale, 2016), 352 pages, ages 4–6

Holman Illustrated Bible Dictionary for Kids (Holman Reference, 2010), 224 pages, ages 5–10

The Action Bible Handbook (David C. Cook, 2013), 224 pages, ages 8–12

Geography Books

Almost all Bibles (especially study Bibles) now contain excellent full-color maps you can use to teach your child basic Bible geography. But if you or your children are interested in more in-depth geographic study, check out these two resources:

Zondervan Atlas of the Bible by Carl G. Rasmussen (Zondervan, 2010), 304 pages, older teens to adults

The New Moody Atlas of the Bible by Barry J. Beitzel (Moody, 2009), 304 pages, older teens to adults

Bible Trivia Books

Trivia includes "details, considerations, or pieces of information of little importance or value," so there should be no category known as Bible trivia.[2] But despite the misleading use of the term, books on Bible trivia can help children learn about Scripture. Here are a few worth considering.

The Everything Kids Bible Trivia Book by Kathi Wagner (Everything, 2004), 144 pages, ages 7–12

Bible Trivia for Kids by Steve and Becky Miller (Harvest House, 1999), 168 pages, ages 9–12

The One Year Book of Bible Trivia for Kids by Katrina Cassel (Tyndale, 2013), ages 10–14

Notes

Why This Book Is Dedicated to *The Boy Scout Handbook*

1. Paul Fussell, *The Boy Scout Handbook and Other Observations* (Oxford, UK: Oxford University Press, 1985), 4.

Chapter 1: How to Learn So You Can Teach

1. Mortimer Adler, *How to Read a Book* (New York, NY: Simon & Schuster, 972), 49.

2. David L. Goodstein, "Richard P. Feynman, Teacher," *Physics Today* 42, no. 2 (February 1989): 75.

Chapter 2: How to Prepare Your Child to Read the Bible

1. Tony Reinke, *Lit!: A Christian Guide to Reading Books* (Wheaton, IL: Crossway, 2011), Kindle edition.

2. Adler co-authored a revision with Charles Van Doren (New York, NY: Touchstone, 1972).

Chapter 3: How to Read the Bible (Elementary)

1. Scott Steltzer, "How God's World Enriches My Experience of God's Word," *The Gospel Coalition*, May 24, 2017, https://www.thegospelcoalition.org/article/how-gods-world-enriches-my-experience-of-gods-word.

2. BibleHub.com, "Bible Weights and Measures," http://biblehub.com/weights-and-measures.

3. BibleHub.com, "Weights and Measures."

4. BibleHub.com, "Weights and Measures."

Chapter 4: How to Read the Bible (Advanced)

1. Cited in Bob Smietana, "Study: Young Bible Readers More Likely to Be Faithful Adults," *Baptist Press*, October 17, 2017, http://www.bpnews.net/49732.

2. John Piper, "The Golden Rule in Bible Reading," *Desiring God*, https://www.desiringgod.org/the-golden-rule-in-bible-reading.

3. R.C. Sproul, "Get a Basic Overview of the Bible," Ligonier Ministries, January 1, 2018, https://www.ligonier.org/blog/get-basic-overview-bible.

4. Robert L. Foster, "On Recognizing Genre in the Bible," *Society of Biblical Literature*, http://www.sbl-site.org/assets/pdfs/TBRecognizingGenre_RF.pdf.

5. For more information, see Joe Carter, *NIV Lifehacks Bible* (Grand Rapids, MI: Zondervan, 2016), 629.

6. *NIV Proclamation Bible* (Grand Rapids, MI: Zondervan, 2011), Kindle edition.

7. Jen Wilkin, "What Student Ministry Really Needs? Homework," *Christianity Today*, November 27, 2017, http://www.christianitytoday.com/ct/2017/december/wilkin-student-ministry-really-needs-bible-homework.html.

Chapter 5: How to See Jesus in the Old Testament

1. "Typology Versus Allegory," *Ligonier Ministries*, http://www.ligonier.org/learn/devotionals/typology-versus-allegory.

2. David Murray, *Jesus on Every Page*. (Grand Rapids, MI: Thomas Nelson, 2013), Kindle edition.

3. For more information, see Joe Carter, *NIV Lifehacks Bible* (Grand Rapids, MI: Zondervan, 2016), 1276.

4. Carter, *NIV Lifehacks Bible*, 1276.

5. Nancy Guthrie, *Lamb of God* (Wheaton, IL: Crossway, 2012), Kindle edition.

6. Joe Rigney, "Where Do We Find Jesus in the Old Testament?," *Desiring God*, August 12, 2011, https://www.desir inggod.org/articles/where-do-we-find-jesus-in-the-old-testament.

Chapter 6: How to Study the Bible

1. David Mathis "Basics for How to Study the Bible," *Desiring God*, https://www.desiringgod.org/basics-for -how-to-study-the-bible.

2. Precept Ministries International, "Know God's Word," https://www.precept.org/know-gods-word.

3. John Piper, "How to Read the Bible for Yourself," *Desiring God*, March 17, 2015, https://www.desiringgod.org/ articles/how-to-read-the-bible-for-yourself.

4. Precept Ministries International, "Know God's Word."

5. Precept Ministries International, "Know God's Word."

Chapter 7: How to Interpret the Bible

1. Craig Keener, "The Importance of Context in Bible study," *Bible Background*, April 16, 2012, http://www.craig keener.com/the-importance-of-context-in-bible-study.

2. Wayne McDill, "7 Principles of Biblical Interpretation," Lifeway Pastors, March 12, 2014, http://www.lifeway .com/pastors/2014/03/12/7-principles-of-biblical-interpretation.

3. John MacArthur, "How Should We Interpret the Bible?," *Grace to You*, August 25, 2013, https://www.gty.org/ library/sermons-library/90-463/how-should-we-interpret-the-bible.

4. Sara Wallace, "How to Teach Kids to Understand the Bible," *The Gospel Coalition*, October 13, 2017, https:// www.thegospelcoalition.org/article/how-to-teach-kids-to-understand-the-bible.

Chapter 8: How to Apply Scripture to Your Life

1. David Powlison, "Reading the Bible for Personal Application," in *Understanding Scripture*, ed. Wayne Grudem, C. John Collins, and Thomas R. Schreiner (Wheaton, IL: Crossway, 2012), Kindle edition.

2. Jon Bloom, "The Most Repeated Command in the Bible," *Desiring God*, November 21, 2017, https://www.desir inggod.org/articles/the-most-repeated-command-in-the-bible.

3. Powlison, "Reading the Bible for Personal Application."

4. For more information, see Joe Carter, *NIV Lifehacks Bible* (Grand Rapids, MI: Zondervan, 2016), 1069.

5. James Gustafson, *From Christ to the World* (Grand Rapids, MI: Eerdmans, 1994), 23.

6. See Proverbs 23:20-21,29-35; Isaiah 5:11; 28:7; Matthew 24:48-49; Galatians 5:21; Ephesians 5:18; 1 Peter 5:8.

7. Cass R. Sunstein, "On Analogical Reasoning," *Harvard Law Review* 106 (1993): 741-91 at 743.

8. Dallas Willard, *The Divine Conspiracy* (San Francisco, CA: HarperOne, 2009), Kindle edition.

9. Sara Wallace, "How to Teach Kids to Understand the Bible," *The Gospel Coalition*, October 13, 2017, https:// www.thegospelcoalition.org/article/how-to-teach-kids-to-understand-the-bible.

10. See Matthew 4:10; 6:24; 15:8-9,19-20; Mark 10:11-12,19; Acts 17:29-30; Romans 7:7; 13:9; 1 Corinthians 6:9; Ephesians 4:25,28; 6:1-3; Hebrews 4:9.

Chapter 9: How to Meditate on God's Word

1. Douglas Groothuis, "Dangerous Meditations," *Christianity Today*, November 1, 2004.

2. John Starke, "Meditation and Communion with God," *The Gospel Coalition*, November 9, 2012, https://www .thegospelcoalition.org/reviews/meditation_and_communion_with_god/.

3. Jean Fleming, *Feeding Your Soul: A Quiet Time Handbook* (Colorado Springs, CO: NavPress, 2014), Kindle edition.

4. "The Joseph Hall Questions," *Biblical Spirituality*, http://biblicalspirituality.org/wp-content/uploads/2011/02/JosephHallQuestions.ppt.

Chapter 11: How to Memorize Entire Books of the Bible

1. Andrew Davis, "An Approach to Extended Memorization of Scripture," *Scripture Memory Fellowship*, October 3, 2017, https://scripturememory.com/downloadables/andrewdavis.pdf.

Chapter 12: How to Read the Bible

1. This step is adapted from Don Whitney's "Bible Reading Record," http://biblicalspirituality.org/bible-reading.

2. This step is adapted from "The Bible Reading Plan for Shirkers and Slackers," http://ransomfellowship.org/article/bible-reading-program-for-slackers-shirkers/.

Chapter 13: How to Memorize the Biblical Narrative

1. Graeme Goldsworthy, *The Goldsworthy Trilogy* (Crownhill, UK: Paternoster, 2001), Kindle edition.

2. R.C. Sproul, "Make No Graven Image," Ligonier Ministries, http://www.ligonier.org/learn/devotionals/make-no-graven-image.

3. *Rhetorica ad Herennium* 3.16-24. English translation by Harry Caplan (Loeb, 1954), http://www.laits.utexas.edu/memoria/Ad_Herennium_Passages.html.

Chapter 14: How to Pray

1. Tim Keller, *Prayer: Experiencing Awe and Intimacy with God* (New York, NY: Penguin, 2014), Kindle edition.

2. Donald S. Whitney, *Spiritual Disciplines for the Christian Life* (Colorado Springs, CO: NavPress, 2014), Kindle edition.

3. For more information, see Joe Carter, *NIV Lifehacks Bible* (Grand Rapids, MI: Zondervan, 2016), 1253.

4. Graeme Goldsworthy, *The Goldsworthy Trilogy* (Crownhill, UK: Paternoster, 2001), Kindle edition.

Chapter 15: How to Be Obedient to God

1. Stephen J. Cole, "Why Jesus Hates Legalism," Bible.org, June 12, 2013, https://bible.org/seriespage/lesson-57-why-jesus-hates-legalism-luke-1137-54.

2. For more information, see Joe Carter, *NIV Lifehacks Bible* (Grand Rapids, MI: Zondervan, 2016), 345.

3. William Law, *A Serious Call to a Devout and Holy Life*, https://www.ccel.org/ccel/law/serious_call.html.

4. For more information, see Joe Carter, *NIV Lifehacks Bible* (Grand Rapids, MI: Zondervan, 2016), 345.

5. John Piper, "Parents, Require Obedience of Your Children," *Desiring God*, October 29, 2013, https://www.desiringgod.org/articles/parents-require-obedience-of-your-children.

Chapter 16: How to Overcome Sin

1. John Owen, *Overcoming Sin and Temptation* (Wheaton, IL: Crossway, 2006), Kindle edition.

2. R.C. Sproul, "When Jesus Says, 'Be Ye Perfect as Your Father in Heaven Is Perfect,' Does That Mean We Can Attain Perfection, and Should We?," Ligonier Ministries, https://www.ligonier.org/learn/qas/when-jesus-says-be-ye-perfect-your-father-heaven-p.

3. For more information, see Joe Carter, *NIV Lifehacks Bible* (Grand Rapids, MI: Zondervan, 2016), 1418.

4. The following quotes are from Tim Challies, "9 Steps to Putting That Sin to Death," Challies.com, January 15, 2015, http://www.challies.com/reading-classics-together/9-steps-to-putting-sin-to-death.

5. John MacArthur, "Is a Temptation Also a Trial?," *Grace to You*, May 8, 2017, https://www.gty.org/library/bibleqnas-library/QA0300/is-a-temptation-also-a-trial.

6. MacArthur, "Is Temptation Also a Trial?"

7. For more information, see Joe Carter, *NIV Lifehacks Bible*, 1418.

Chapter 17: How to Develop Trust in God

1. Herbert Lockyer, *All the Promises of the Bible* (Grand Rapids, MI: Zondervan, 1962), Kindle edition.

2. Barnabas Piper, "You Can't Claim a Promise," BarnabasPiper.com, September 2, 2016, http://www.barnabaspiper.com/2014/04/you-cant-claim-a-promise.html.

3. John Ortberg, *If You Want to Walk on Water, You've Got to Get Out of the Boat* (Grand Rapids, MI: Zondervan, 2008), Kindle edition.

Chapter 18: How to Handle Criticism

1. Sue Shellenbarger, "How to Take Criticism Well," *Wall Street Journal*, June 18, 2014, https://www.wsj.com/articles/how-to-take-criticism-well-1403046866.

Chapter 20: How to Say You're Sorry

1. Katie Heany, "The Apology Critics Who Want to Teach You How to Say You're Sorry," *New York Magazine*, June, 8, 2017, http://nymag.com/scienceofus/2017/06/these-apology-critics-want-to-teach-you-how-to-say-sorry.html.

2. JoEllen Poon, "When 'I'm Sorry' Isn't Enough: How to Apologize Properly," *Verily*, August 5, 2014, https://verilymag.com/2014/08/how-to-apologize-properly.

Chapter 21: How to Forgive

1. Chris Brauns, *Unpacking Forgiveness: Biblical Answers for Complex Questions and Deep Wounds* (Wheaton, IL: Crossway, 2008), Kindle edition.

2. John Stott, *Confess Your Sins: The Way of Reconciliation* (Grand Rapids, MI: Eerdmans, 1964), Kindle edition.

3. For more information, see Joe Carter, *NIV Lifehacks Bible* (Grand Rapids, MI: Zondervan, 2016), 60.

4. Rose Sweet, "Why Do We Find It So Hard to Forgive?," *Focus on the Family*, http://www.focusonthefamily.com/marriage/divorce-and-infidelity/forgiveness-and-restoration/forgiveness-what-it-is-and-what-it-isnt.

5. Sweet, "Why Do We Find It So Hard to Forgive?"

6. "The Young Peacemaker," Peacemaker Ministries, http://peacemaker.net/young-peacemaker.

7. "The Young Peacemaker."

8. Ken Sande, *The Peacemaker* (Grand Rapids, MI: Baker Books, 2004), Kindle edition.

Chapter 22: How to Develop Your Conscience

1. John MacArthur, *The Book on Leadership* (Nashville, TN: Thomas Nelson, 2004), 78.

Chapter 23: How to Know God's Will for Your Life

1. R.C. Sproul, *Essential Truths of the Christian Faith* (Carol Springs, IL: Tyndale House, 1992), Kindle edition.

2. Kevin DeYoung, *Just Do Something: A Liberating Approach to Finding God's Will* (Chicago, IL: Moody, 2009), Kindle edition.

3. DeYoung, *Just Do Something*, Kindle edition.

4. Karl Vaters, "Finding God's Will for Your Life Is Easier Than You Think," *Christianity Today*, September 12, 2016, http://www.christianitytoday.com/karl-vaters/2016/september/finding-gods-will-for-your-life-is-easier -than-you-think.html.

5. David Sills, "8 Essential Components for Discerning God's Will," *Southern Equip*, http://www.sbts.edu/ blogs/2015/02/17/8-essential-components-for-discerning-gods-will.

6. For more information, see Joe Carter, *NIV Lifehacks Bible* (Grand Rapids, MI: Zondervan, 2016), 1156.

Chapter 24: How to Make Better Decisions

1. Sheena Iyengar, "How to Make Choosing Easier," TED.com, https://www.ted.com/talks/sheena_iyengar _choosing_what_to_choose/transcript#t-64567.

2. This model is derived in part from two sources: Peter F. Drucker, "The Effective Decision," *Harvard Business Review*, January 1967, https://hbr.org/1967/01/the-effective-decision; and Gary T. Meadors, *Decision Making God's Way* (Grand Rapids, MI: Baker Books, 2003), Kindle edition.

Chapter 25: How to Develop Biblical Discernment

1. Tim Challies, *The Discipline of Spiritual Discernment* (Wheaton, IL: Crossway, 2007), Kindle edition.

2. John MacArthur, "What Is Biblical Discernment and Why Is It Important?," *Grace to You*, https://www.gty.org/ library/questions/QA138/what-is-biblical-discernment-and-why-is-it-important.

3. Sinclair Ferguson, *In Christ Alone* (Mary, Florida: Reformation Trust, 2007), Kindle edition.

4. Ferguson, *In Christ Alone*.

5. "Teaching Children Discernment," blog post, *gotQuestions? Kidz*, http://www.gqkidz.org/parents/blog/ Teaching-Discernment.php.

Chapter 26: How to Sleep

1. John Ortberg, *The Life You've Always Wanted: Spiritual Disciplines for Ordinary People* (Grand Rapids, MI: Zondervan, 2002), Kindle edition.

2. Jessica Schmerler, "Q&A: Why Is Blue Light before Bedtime Bad for Sleep?," *Scientific American*, September 1, 2015.

3. Travis Bradberry, "Caffeine: The Silent Killer of Success," *Forbes*, August 12, 2012.

4. Markham Heid, "You Asked: Is Sleeping in a Cold Room Better for You?," *Time* magazine, November 26, 2014.

Chapter 27: How to Manage Stress

1. "Stressors," *Centre for Study on Human Stress*, http://humanstress.ca/stress/what-is-stress/stressors.

2. "Stressors," *Centre for Study on Human Stress*.

3. "What Is Stress?," *Stress Management Society*, http://www.stress.org.uk/what-is-stress.

4. Dr. Chloe Carmichael, "Eustress: The Stress You Actually Need," *U.S. News & World Reports*, September 12, 2017, https://health.usnews.com/health-care/for-better/articles/2017-09-12/eustress-the-stress-you-actually-need.

5. Richard Swenson, *Margin* (Colorado Springs: NavPress, 2014), Kindle edition.

6. Cited in Esther Entin, "All Work and No Play: Why Your Kids Are More Anxious, Depressed," *The Atlantic*, October 12, 2011, https://www.theatlantic.com/health/archive/2011/10/all-work-and-no-play-why-your -kids-are-more-anxious-depressed/246422.

7. Bonnie Singleton, "Box Breathing Technique," *Arizona Central*, https://healthyliving.azcentral.com/box -breathing-technique-11421.html.

Chapter 28: How to Handle Loss and Grief

1. Russell Friedman, "The Best Grief Definition You Will Find," The Grief Recovery Method, http://blog.griefre coverymethod.com/blog/2013/06/best-grief-definition-you-will-find.

2. Elizabeth Groves, "Grief and the Christian," Ligonier Ministries, January 1, 2016, https://www.ligonier.org/learn/articles/grief-and-christian.

3. Claudia Jarrett, *Helping Children Cope with Separation and Loss* (Cambridge, MA: Harvard Common Press, 1994), Kindle edition.

4. Jeanine Bozeman, "Helping Children Cope with Grief," LifeWay, https://www.lifeway.com/en/articles/children-and-grief.

Chapter 29: How to Deal with Fear and Anxiety

1. Cited in R.C. Sproul, "What Does It Mean to Fear God?," Ligonier Ministries, http://www.ligonier.org/blog/what-does-it-mean-fear-god.

2. Philipp Melanchthon, *Loci Theologici Recens Recogniti*, 1543, https://books.google.com/books?id=ghw8AAAAcAAJ.

3. For more information, see Joe Carter, *NIV Lifehacks Bible* (Grand Rapids, MI: Zondervan, 2016), 743.

4. David Powlison, *Overcoming Anxiety* (Greensboro, NC: New Growth Press, 2012), Kindle edition.

Chapter 30: How to Develop a Healthy Body Image

1. National Eating Disorders Association, "What Are Eating Disorders?," https://www.nationaleatingdisorders.org/get-facts-eating-disorders.

2. Jamie Santa Cruz, "Body-Image Pressure Increasingly Affects Boys," *The Atlantic*, March 10, 2014, https://www.theatlantic.com/health/archive/2014/03/body-image-pressure-increasingly-affects-boys/283897/.

3. Centers for Disease Control, "Body Measurements," https://www.cdc.gov/nchs/fastats/body-measurements.htm.

4. Lauren Effron, "Fashion Models: By the Numbers," *ABC News*, September 19, 2011, http://abcnews.go.com/blogs/lifestyle/2011/09/fashion-models-by-the-numbers/.

5. K.P. Arbour and K.A. Martin Ginis, "Effects of Exposure to Muscular and Hypermuscular Media Images on Young Men's Muscularity Dissatisfaction and Body Dissatisfaction," *Body Image* 3 (2006), 153-61.

6. Heather L. Jacobson, M. Elizabeth Lewis Hall, Tamara L. Anderson, and Michele M. Willingham, "Temple or Prison: Religious Beliefs and Attitudes Toward the Body," *Journal of Religion and Health* 55, no. 6 (December 2016), 2154-73.

7. Sharon Hodde Miller, "Why Pastors Should Preach About Body Image," *Christianity Today*, July 16, 2014, http://www.christianitytoday.com/women/2014/july/why-pastors-should-preach-about-body-image.html.

Chapter 31: How to Develop Godly Grit

1. Angela Lee Duckworth, "The Key to Success? Grit," *TED Talks Education*, http://www.ted.com/talks/angela_lee_duckworth_the_key_to_success_grit.

2. For more information, see Joe Carter, *NIV Lifehacks Bible* (Grand Rapids, MI: Zondervan, 2016), 1400.

3. Jon Bloom, "True Grit," *Desiring God*, August 15, 2014, https://www.desiringgod.org/articles/true-grit.

4. James Hamblin, "Don't Call Your Kids Smart," *The Atlantic*, June 30, 2015, https://www.theatlantic.com/education/archive/2015/06/the-s-word/397205/.

Chapter 32: How to Tame Your Tongue

1. Stephen R. Covey, "Habit 5: Seek First to Understand, Then to Be Understood," StephenCovey.com, https://www.stephencovey.com/7habits/7habits-habit5.php.

Chapter 33: How to Develop Virtuous Habits

1. For more information, see Joe Carter, *NIV Lifehacks Bible* (Grand Rapids, MI: Zondervan, 2016), 759.

2. Charles Duhigg, *The Power of Habit* (New York, NY: Random House, 2014), Kindle edition.

Chapter 34: How to Change Negative Habits

1. John Wesley, "On Dress," http://wesley.nnu.edu/john-wesley/the-sermons-of-john-wesley-1872-edition/sermon-88-on-dress.

2. James Clear, "How Long Does It Actually Take to Form a New Habit? (Backed by Science)," JamesClear.com, https://jamesclear.com/new-habit.

Chapter 35: How to Look at Art

1. Nicholas Wolterstorff, *Art in Action* (Grand Rapids, MI: Eerdmans), Kindle edition.

2. Francis Schaeffer, *Art and the Bible* (Downers Grove, IL: InterVarsity Press, 1973).

3. Calvin Seerveld, *A Christian Critique of Art and Literature* (Sioux Center, IA: Dordt College Press, 1995), Kindle edition.

4. H.R. Rookmaaker, *Modern Art and the Death of Culture* (Wheaton, IL: Crossway, 1991), 4.

5. Cited in Rookmaaker, *Modern Art and the Death of Culture*, 4.

6. Kit Messham-Muir, "Three Simple Steps to Understand Art: Look, See, Think," *The Conversation*, October 22, 2014, http://theconversation.com/three-simple-steps-to-understand-art-look-see-think-33020.

7. Amelia Gentleman, "Smile, Please," *The Guardian*, https://www.theguardian.com/artanddesign/2004/oct/19/art.france.

8. Kit Messham-Muir, "Three questions not to ask about art—and four to ask instead," *The Conversation*, August 21, 2014, https://theconversation.com/three-questions-not-to-ask-about-art-and-four-to-ask-instead-29830.

9. Fred Sanders, "How to Look at Art," *The Scriptorium Daily*, July 16, 2007, http://scriptoriumdaily.com/how-to-look-at-art.

Chapter 37: How to Watch a Movie

1. "Film Grammar," Wikipedia, https://en.wikipedia.org/wiki/Film_grammar.

2. Roger Ebert, "How to Read a Film," RogerEbert.com, https://www.rogerebert.com/rogers-journal/how-to-read-a-movie.

3. These elements and questions are adapted from Tyler Schirado's "How to Analyze a Movie: A Step-by-step Guide," *San Diego Film Festival*, http://sdfilmfest.com/how-to-analyze-a-movie-step-by-step-guide-to-reviewing-films-from-a-screeners-point-of-view/.

4. Schirado, "How to Analyze a Movie."

5. William D. Romanowski, *Eyes Wide Open* (Grand Rapids, MI: Brazos Press, 2001), Kindle edition.

6. Gene Veith, "The Defining Element in Christian Art," GeneVeith.com, http://www.geneveith.com/2012/04/30/the-defining-element-in-christian-art.

Chapter 38: How to Consume the News

1. Robinson Meyer, "How Many Stories Do Newspapers Publish Per Day?," *The Atlantic*, https://www.theatlantic.com/technology/archive/2016/05/how-many-stories-do-newspapers-publish-per-day/483845.

2. C. John Sommerville, "Why the News Makes Us Dumb," *First Things*, October 1991, https://www.firstthings.com/article/1991/10/why-the-news-makes-us-dumb.

3. C. John Sommerville, *How the News Makes Us Dumb* (Downers Grove, IL: InterVarsity Press, 2009), Kindle edition.

4. Neil Postman, *How to Watch TV News* (New York, NY: Penguin Group, 1992), Kindle edition.

5. Cited in Sommerville, *How the News Makes Us Dumb*, 54.

6. Neil Postman, *Conscientious Objections* (New York, NY: Random House, 1988), Kindle edition.

7. Sommerville, *How the News Makes Us Dumb*, 54.

Chapter 39: How to Study

1. Francis Bacon, *The Advancement of Learning*, 1605, https://www.gutenberg.org/files/5500/5500-h/5500-h.htm.

2. "Study," Dictionary.com, http://www.dictionary.com/browse/study.

3. Jim Roth, "The Curve of Forgetting," http://ol.scc.spokane.edu/jroth/Courses/English%2094-study%20skills/MASTER%20DOCS%20and%20TESTS/Curve%20of%20Forgetting.htm.

4. "Curve of Forgetting," *University of Waterloo*, https://uwaterloo.ca/campus-wellness/curve-forgetting.

5. Roth, "The Curve of Forgetting."

6. Jenny Anderson, "A Stanford Researcher's 15-Minute Study Hack Lifts B+ Students into the As," *Quartz*, May 9, 2017, https://qz.com/978273/a-stanford-professors-15-minute-study-hack-improves-test-grades-by-a-third-of-a-grade.

Chapter 40: How to Become a Better Learner

1. Ulrich Boser, *Learn Better* (New York, NY: Rodale Books, 2017).

2. Ulrich Boser, "The Best Way to Learn Is Taking a Mixed Up Approach to Practice," *Quartz*, December 22, 2017, https://qz.com/1163392/the-best-way-to-learn-is-taking-a-mixed-up-approach-to-practice.

Chapter 41: How to Memorize Almost Anything

1. Mary Carruthers, *The Book of Memory: A Study of Memory in Medieval Culture* (Cambridge, UK: Cambridge University Press, 2008), Kindle edition.

2. Ed Cooke, *Remember, Remember: Learn the Stuff You Thought You Never Could* (New York, NY: Penguin, 2008), Kindle edition.

3. Thomas Aquinas, *Summa Theologica*, 1274, Christian Classics Ethereal Library, https://www.ccel.org/ccel/aquinas/summa.html.

4. Harry Lorayne and Jerry Lucas, *The Memory Book: The Classic Guide to Improving Your Memory at Work, at School, and at Play* (New York, NY: Ballantine Books, 2012), Kindle edition.

5. Cicero, *De Oratore*, book 2, section 88, 351-54, E.W. Sutton and H. Rackham, tr., Loeb Classical Library.

Chapter 42: How to Focus

1. "Thinking Skills: Focus," *Learning Works for Kids*, http://learningworksforkids.com/skills/focus.

2. "Attention-Deficit / Hyperactivity Disorder (ADHD)," *Centers for Disease Control and Prevention*, https://www.cdc.gov/ncbddd/adhd/data.html.

Chapter 43: How to Handle Conflict

1. Ronald Reagan, "Address at Commencement Exercises at Eureka College in IL," *The American Presidency Project*, May 9, 1982, http://www.presidency.ucsb.edu/ws/index.php?pid=42501.

2. Steven J. Cole, "Resolving Conflicts God's Way (James 4:7-10)," Bible.org, https://bible.org/seriespage/lesson-16-resolving-conflicts-god%E2%80%99s-way-james-47-10.

3. Ken Sande, *The Peacemaker* (Grand Rapids, MI: Baker Books, 2004), Kindle edition.

Chapter 44: How to Deal with Bullying and Harassment

1. "Effects of Bullying," *StopBullying.gov*, https://www.stopbullying.gov/at-risk/effects/index.html.
2. "What Is Bullying," *StopBullying.gov*, https://www.stopbullying.gov/what-is-bullying/roles-kids-play/index.html.
3. C.P. Bradshaw, A.L. Sawyer, and L.M. O'Brennan, "Bullying and Peer Victimization at School: Perceptual Differences Between Students and School Staff," *School Psychology Review*, 36(3), 361-382, 2007.
4. M.M. Tofi and D.P. Farrington, "Effectiveness of School-Based Programs to Reduce Bullying: A Systematic and Meta-analytic Review," *Journal of Experimental Criminology*, 7(1), 27-56, 2007.
5. Walt Larimore, "The Truth About Bullying," Crosswalk.com, https://www.crosswalk.com/family/parenting/the-truth-about-bullying-1245701.html.
6. "The Roles Kids Play in Bullying," *StopBullying.gov*, https://www.stopbullying.gov/what-is-bullying/roles-kids-play/index.html.
7. D.L. Hawkins, D. Pepler, and W.M. Craig, "Peer Interventions in Playground Bullying," *Social Development*, 10, 512-527, 2001.

Chapter 45: How to Handle Family Conflict

1. Richard Pratt, Jr., "Broken Homes in the Bible," Ligonier Ministries, December 1, 2011, https://www.ligonier.org/learn/articles/broken-homes-in-the-bible/.
2. Quoted in Po Bronson and Ashley Merryman, *NurtureShock: New Thinking About Children* (New York, NY: Hatchette Book Group, 2009), Kindle edition.
3. Ilan Shrira and Joshua D. Foster, "When Parents Play Favorite," *Psychology Today*, January 10, 2009, https://www.psychologytoday.com/blog/the-narcissus-in-all-us/200901/when-parents-play-favorites.
4. Bruce Feiler, *The Secrets of Happy Families* (New York, NY: HarperCollins, 2013), Kindle edition.
5. Hildy S. Ross and Marysia J. Lazinski, "Parent Mediation Empowers Sibling Conflict Resolution," *Early Education and Development* 25:2, pages 259-275, 2014.
6. Quoted in Feiler, *The Secrets of Happy Families*.
7. Elaine Shpungin, "3 Steps That Transform Sibling Conflict into Sibling Camaraderie," *Psychology Today*, October 8, 2010, https://www.psychologytoday.com/blog/peacemeal/201010/3-steps-transform-sibling-conflict-sibling-camaraderie.

Chapter 46: How to Handle Peer Pressure

1. "Peer Pressure," *Merriam-Webster Dictionary*, https://www.merriam-webster.com/dictionary/peer%20pressure.
2. "Eddie Haskell," Wikipedia, https://en.wikipedia.org/wiki/Eddie_Haskell.
3. "Parents Influence Teens' Drinking Decisions: Survey," Partnership for Drug-Free Kids, https://drugfree.org/learn/drug-and-alcohol-news/parents-influence-teens-drinking-decisions-survey.

Chapter 47: How to Start a Conversation About the Gospel

1. For more information, see Joe Carter, *NIV Lifehacks Bible* (Grand Rapids, MI: Zondervan, 2016), 1284.

Chapter 48: How to Defend the Faith

1. Tim Keller, "In Defense of Apologetics," *The Gospel Coalition*, August 5, 2012, https://www.thegospelcoalition.org/article/in-defense-of-apologetics.

2. Paul Rezkalla, "The Great Commission for Apologetics," *The Gospel Coalition*, July 11, 2014, https://www.thegospelcoalition.org/article/the-great-commission-for-apologetics. *July 11,4*

3. Greg Koukl, *Tactics* (Grand Rapids, MI: Zondervan, 2009), 51.

Chapter 49: How to Tell a Bible Story

1. John B. Polhill, *Acts*, vol. 26, *The New American Commentary* (Nashville, TN: Broadman & Holman Publishers, 1992), Kindle edition.

2. J.O. Terry, *Basic Bible Storying*, Amazon Digital Services.

3. Terry, *Basic Bible Storying*.

4. Jack Day, "How to Tell a Bible Story," http://gbod.org.s3.amazonaws.com/legacy/kintera/entry_5469/19/HOWTOTELL.PDF.

Chapter 50: How to Share the Gospel

1. Donald Whitney, "How to Measure Basic Gospel Literacy," *The Center for Biblical Spirituality*, http://biblical spirituality.org/how-to-measure-basic-gospel-literacy.

2. Simon Gathercole, "The Gospel of Paul and the Gospel of the Kingdom," in *God's Power to Save*, ed. Chris Green (Downers Grove: IL: Apollos/InterVarsity Press, 2006), Kindle edition.

3. John Piper, "At What Point Should I Share the Gospel with My Neighbor?," *Desiring God*, https://www.desir inggod.org/interviews/at-what-point-should-i-share-the-gospel-with-my-neighbor.

4. Mark Dever, *The Gospel and Personal Evangelism* (Wheaton, IL: Crossway, 2007), 82.

5. Shane Raynor, "5 Evangelism Barriers (and How to Deal with Them)," *Ministry Matters*, September 17, 2013, http://www.ministrymatters.com/all/entry/4259/5-evangelism-barriers-and-how-to-deal-with-them.

Recommended Resources

1. Rachel Tiemeyer, "7 Must-Have Children's Bibles for All Ages (And How to Avoid All the Bad Ones)," *Thriving Home*, http://thrivinghomeblog.com/2014/08/7-excellent-childrens-bibles-ages.

2. "Trivia," *Oxford Dictionary*.

About the Author

Joe Carter is an editor for the Gospel Coalition, an educator, and a 15-year Marine Corps veteran. He has held several positions in the publishing field and has been cited in numerous publications, including the *New York Times,* the *Wall Street Journal,* and the *Washington Post.*

To learn more about Harvest House books and
to read sample chapters, visit our website:

www.harvesthousepublishers.com

HARVEST HOUSE PUBLISHERS
EUGENE, OREGON

More Great Books for Parents from Harvest House Publishers

Are You Prepared to Talk with Your Child About...?

Discussing difficult topics with kids has never been easy, but in today's world, it's more difficult than ever. Gay marriage, terrorist attacks, pornography, police shootings, and yes, sex, are just some of the complex issues children will encounter in our current culture. When your child asks questions, will you have answers?

Tough Stuff Parenting will equip you to have thoughtful, age-appropriate conversations with your child. The biblically based wisdom and practical tools you'll find inside will help you confidently engage your kid in meaningful dialogue. And when questions arise, your child will look to you first for answers instead of friends or the internet.

Make a lasting connection with your kid by learning how to effectively discuss life's most complicated topics.

A Healthy View of Sexuality Starts with God

God created sex to be good. But our culture is drifting away from a biblical worldview and is promoting an unhealthy view of sexuality. The church has taken a defensive approach, giving our kids a long list of "do nots" with few words of hope or redemption.

Do you want something better for your child?

Rediscover God's plan for sexuality and instill a positive perspective of sex and identity in your children. *Mom, Dad...What's Sex?* will equip you to

- help your child learn what God's Word—and today's culture—say about sex
- understand the influence pop culture and social media have on your kid
- share a gospel-centered, hopeful message with your son or daughter

Give your child a healthy view of sexuality grounded in biblical truth—recognizing the gift of intimacy, the reality of brokenness, and the redeeming work of the Savior.

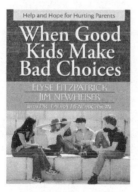

There is perhaps no greater fear in a parent's heart than the thought that a much-loved and well-cared-for child will make bad choices or even become a prodigal.

What are parents to do in such circumstances? Authors Jim Newheiser and Elyse Fitzpatrick speak from years of personal experience as both parents and biblical counselors about how hurting parents can deal with the emotional trauma of when a child goes astray. They offer concrete hope and encouragement along with positive steps parents can take even in the most negative situations.

Includes excellent advice from Dr. Laura Hendrickson regarding medicines commonly prescribed to problem children, and offers questions parents can ask pediatricians before using behavioral medications. A heartfelt and practical guide for parents.

You're deeply committed to helping your kids succeed. But you're concerned—why are so many graduates unprepared to enter the workforce and face life on their own? You're doing your best to raise healthy children, but sometimes you wonder, *am I really helping them?*

Tim Elmore shows you how to avoid twelve critical mistakes parents unintentionally make. He outlines practical and effective parenting skills so you won't fall into common traps, such as...

- making happiness a goal instead of a by-product
- not letting kids struggle or fight for what they believe
- not letting them fail or suffer consequences
- lying about kids' potential—and not exploring their true potential
- giving them what they should earn

Find out why thousands of organizations have sought out Tim Elmore to help them develop young leaders—and how you can improve your parenting skills and help your kids soar.